The Nautical Institute

Mentoring at Sea
The 10 minute challenge

by

Captain André L Le Goubin MA FNI

D1344154

Mentoring at Sea
The 10 minute challenge

by

Captain André L Le Goubin MA FNI

Published by The Nautical Institute
202 Lambeth Road, London SE1 7LQ, England
Tel: +44 (0)20 7928 1351   Fax: +44 (0)20 7401 2817   Web: www.nautinst.org
© The Nautical Institute 2012

Book Editor Paul Bartlett
Author portrait by Rachael V Le Goubin
Images courtesy of Danny Cornelissen (www.portpictures.nl)
Design and typesetting by PMD Visual Communications
Printed in the UK by Geerings Print Ltd

ISBN 978 1 906915 39 1

Foreword

by **Captain Krish Krishnamurthi** FNI

President
The Nautical Institute

Mentoring has been an essential element of sea-going lore for centuries. I daresay the very concept of mentoring had its birth at sea. 'Learning the ropes' is a common phrase that is attributed to this ancient sea-going tradition. For various reasons, it has been relegated to the shadows in the past few decades. That is, until André Le Goubin so elegantly and passionately brought this to the collective consciousness of The Nautical Institute.

André writes this book in a wonderfully easy, conversational style with none of the structured and prescriptive approach that so often tends to draw boundaries around free thought. And therein lies the fundamental difference between training and mentoring. Training transfers underpinning theory and lays down the rules and the laws of things, which is very important in itself. But it is the informal and effortless transfer of experiential skill-sets through artful mentoring that rounds off the competency profile.

Very few of us can look back in time and not remember the names of those few good men and women who have left an indelible imprint on the way we think, speak and act in the course of our work, and indeed, our lives. In that sense, mentors attain immortality and live on through their successors long after they have retired and passed on.

In the last three decades, the shipping industry and the maritime profession have both seen rapid and bewildering changes. We have witnessed fundamental changes in the application of technology. Business and work cultures have transitioned from a national to a multi-national character. In the milieu of globalisation, most small and medium shipowning and management firms have experienced a dilution of their individual brand as they subscribed to the lowest common denominator that international competition seems to demand.

In response to concerns raised about falling professional standards through the political and administrative process, ISM and STCW evolved to create the mitigating structure. But I believe it is up to us professionals and peers to bring the heart into play through mentoring.

André makes a very powerful point that ship safety is greatly enhanced through the mentoring culture. He has sprinkled this book with some excellent case studies of casualties where effective mentoring could have prevented the mishaps. While safety is a noble goal in itself, I'd add that safety and protection of the environment have become genuine drivers of business assurance in niche markets.

Mentoring at Sea

Unlike onboard training, which demands time resource, mentoring is an informal process and is best imparted while engaged in shipboard operations. Most of the challenges and roadblocks are mental and emotional. The author makes a strong case for transcending language and cultural barriers for mentoring to succeed. This is achievable through a top-down corporate culture of nurturing talent, promoting excellence and being intolerant of prejudice and 'whining' about junior officers. Perhaps, 'mentoring potential' is a parameter that should find its way into the performance appraisals of both sea-going officers and shore-based executives.

Fast promotions and reduced sea-time requirements between certificates of competency are sources of concern as they leave very little time to gain enough experiential skills and knowledge. Ironically, with increasing focus on safety, the mean time between incidents or breakdowns has also increased. This, I feel, has only added to the paucity of real life experiences, which are so essential to preparing for ascending responsibilities.

Given the inherent informal and unstructured character of mentoring, it cannot and certainly should not be a statutory or regulated subject. The responsibility to promote and effectively implement mentoring therefore falls on professional peer groups and associations as well as on the responsible corporate citizen.

André provides some very sensible and interesting tools for the mentor. Reflection is such a fabulous tool and so seriously underrated in these days of excessive and mindless chatter on blogs, Twitter, Facebook and such-like. The 10 minute challenge harks back to an ancient philosophy that all the answers to life's greatest challenges lie within us, if only we'd care to search inwards through calm reflection.

Reverse mentoring is another gem that challenges a pre-conceived notion that you need to be a senior pro to qualify as a mentor. Increasingly, the seniors could do well to learn a trick or two from Generation Y, who seem to be gifted with a baffling level of ease and comfort with technology that seems to be denied by the gods to more experienced professionals.

Relevance is another critical tool. You simply can't teach obsolete tricks to any dog, old or new. While we are sentimentally attached to the things that were bread and butter in our time, we need to understand that youngsters will quickly sense that you haven't bothered to update your skills and knowledge over time. This is the starting point of the generation gap.

While I realise the writing of this excellent book on mentoring at sea is the culmination of a most satisfying personal journey for André Le Goubin, it is also the beginning of an equally rewarding journey for all maritime professionals who long to share their hard-won knowledge and skills across the flimsy boundaries and barriers of nations, cultures and regions.

Contents

Dedication

This book is dedicated to all the mentors in my life, past and present, who have helped me get to where I am now. Although many, none did more than Captain J M (Jack) Healy, who recognised my love of the sea at an early age and did so much to teach and encourage me, while I was still a boy. While he has crossed the bar, as have so many others, I hope that this book will continue or resume the process of transferring experiential knowledge at sea by mentoring that was so natural to seafarers like him.

It is also dedicated to my wife Debbie and our children Philip, Rachael and Robert, without whose encouragement, steadfast support and sense of humour, I doubt I would have even attempted much of what I have achieved over our years together.

Finally, it is dedicated, with grateful thanks, to all at The Nautical Institute who have supported and partnered with me through my masters degree studies and encouraged me to continue and develop my research into this book.

Together we can make a difference.

Introduction

Before we start properly, I would like to talk to you about this book and my style of writing. I am not a professional writer and this is not a text book. I am an ordinary mariner who is very concerned about mentoring and who would like to have a conversation with you about it.

Imagine that I have come on board your ship or to your place of work. I am with you on the bridge, or in the machinery control room, for example, having a discussion on how, between us, we can improve life at sea for today's seafarers, by sharing experiential knowledge for the benefit of ourselves and those who will come after us.

We have started chatting about mentoring, as often happens to me. You will have your views and I have mine – I respect that. In this book there will be as many questions as there are answers but that is no different from any conversation that takes place. All I hope is that you will read this and, although you will probably not agree with all of its contents, you will find some of it thought-provoking and be challenged to pass on some of the knowledge you have gained to someone else. For that is what it is all about. If that happens, then I will have achieved my objective.

By way of introduction, let me tell you a little bit about myself. I was born on the island of Sark in the Channel Islands, an island of just three miles by a little more than one. Although I was the son of a baker, it was soon apparent that the 'sea was in my blood' as, by the age of four, I am told, I had decided that I was going to sea. Of course, at that age I was going straight to be the Captain! I never wavered from that desire. From the age of eight, I spent the majority of my spare time with fishermen on board a lobster fishing boat.

In 1973, I passed the 11 plus – an examination enabling me to attend a grammar school in either Guernsey or Jersey. As we lived on a small island accessible only by boat, when the weather was OK, I would have to go away to school to board there. My parents didn't want this and decided that, rather than break up the family, we would all move to Guernsey, a somewhat larger island nine miles from Sark.

Once settled in Guernsey, I again spent my spare time at sea – this time on a small cargo and passenger vessel trading between the islands. Working as a deck boy had the most profound effect on me. I had tuition in the art of old-fashioned seamanship from the Master of the vessel, who was a strict and principled man who was born in 1921. I believe he ran away to sea from Ireland, sometime before the second world war, when just a boy. Today, I still reflect upon those times and regularly use the skills he taught me; skills such as basic shiphandling, meteorology and cargo work. I am trained to a far higher standard in these skills today, but his teachings provided the solid foundation that all else was subsequently built upon.

At the age of 16, I was legally able to 'sign on' and so became a paid member of crew during my school holidays. As ordinary seaman, I obtained my steering certificate, my first merchant navy qualification. In the school summer holidays of 1979, and again in 1980, I signed on as a deckhand aboard a slightly larger coastal vessel trading between the Channel Islands, England and France. How I wish the industry today still allowed youngsters opportunities to go to sea and learn their trade, even before they leave school. The people who taught me those early skills were, in my opinion, true mentors.

Nine years followed sailing deepsea with Cunard Shipping Services. I was lucky, as this was the cargo division and Cunard's wide variety of vessel types gave me a diverse learning experience. But this was the 1980s during the infamous decline of the British merchant navy as we knew it.

By 1989, the fleet was seriously depleted, the voyages were becoming longer and conditions were changing rapidly. So I decided to look for a new job in the ferry trade. Suddenly, I was in the right place at the right time and, at the age of 27, I was offered command of a passenger-carrying hydrofoil. This was probably the steepest learning curve I have ever had to negotiate and – I have to be honest – it wasn't without its 'learning moments'. As I reflect on those times, I have come to realise that although experiences can be good or bad, the knowledge gained from those experiences can only ever be good.

I stayed with the fast ferry trade for nearly 10 years, with the exception of three years working ashore for the local Channel Island government. That time only served to convince me I needed to be at sea, working on ships and with seafarers. By now married with children, I moved to the UK mainland to work on high-speed car and passenger-carrying catamarans crossing the Dover Strait. This gave me a very different perspective on maritime life as I crossed that narrow stretch of water up to six times a day. I had to weave my way through the 300 ships that transit it daily with my vessel travelling at speeds of up to 43.8 knots. That was the fastest I ever travelled – when I was on a brand new 100-metre monohull approaching the port of Calais one fine Sunday morning.

In 1998 the writing was on the wall for the cessation of duty free sales between European Union countries. The ferry company I was working for was largely supported by the revenue from these sales and so I decided it was time to move on.

I had, for a long time, nurtured the idea of becoming a pilot. My grandfather had been a pilot for the Island of Sark, probably the first one, and he had written the syllabus for the pilotage exam I sat so many years later, when Master of a hydrofoil. During my Sark pilotage examination, some of the more elderly Masters on the examination board that day remembered my grandfather well. No pressure then! I passed successfully and the party afterwards was certainly one to remember!

Soon after, I applied to the Port of London Authority and a chance meeting with a pilot at a Nautical Institute meeting enabled me to take a trip up the Thames and gain introductions to all the right people. Following successful interviews, I joined the PLA in 1999 as a trainee pilot.

If you had shown me then how my dining room table would look in six months' time, covered and weighed down with the charts, publications and paperwork of everything I would need to learn to become an authorised pilot, I would have said that I was not capable of absorbing that amount of information. As it was I did manage it, but it was hard work and I can honestly say I have never studied so hard in my life. However, the feeling when I officially became pilot number 241 made it all worthwhile.

I loved that job – even the study that took me through from Class 4 to Class 1. I particularly enjoyed piloting bigger and deeper draught ships. However, after a few years my wife and I became restless. We dreamed of moving to somewhere where the sun shines a lot more than it does in the UK. We had become very disillusioned with our way of life, the rising taxation and, in our opinion, falling standards. But, if I was honest, it had as much to do with the lack of sunshine. So there I was one morning, having breakfast and flicking through the latest *Seaways*, the publication of The Nautical Institute, of which I have been a member for many years. I saw an advert for a marine consultant to join a worldwide company of marine and engineering consultants with an expanding office in Florida, work visa included.

We had visited Florida for a number of years and we loved the place so I decided to research the company. To my great surprise I discovered one of my old maritime college friends ran their Norwegian office. I applied for the job, got it, obtained the visa, and within five months, we had packed everything into a 20-foot container and emigrated to Florida!

This sounds so simple when you put it down on paper but it was one of the biggest decisions of my life. Most people were supportive, some people thought we were daft and some thought that I must have done something terribly wrong to be leaving a job that is considered by most mariners to be the pinnacle of a seagoing career. I can only agree with all those sentiments (except that I had not in fact done anything wrong!). But imagine if, a few years later, we were still in the UK and playing the 'what-if' game.

Sometimes you just have to bite the bullet and go in what your heart says is the right direction. However it wasn't easy and I missed being a pilot, but the US turned out to be everything we had hoped it would be. It is not perfect. The way of life certainly wouldn't suit everyone and how I miss my real fish and chips. But it suits us and I can only hope it stays that way.

I spent two years in South Florida and then moved to the company head office in Houston where I stayed for the next six years. Well actually, during that time, I could be anywhere, as I spent much of my time away from home on board ships and offshore, engaged in many marine activities but primarily marine accident investigation and casualty work in all its guises.

Very recently, the call of the sea has become too strong again and I have left the consultancy and returned to seafaring, as a mooring master in the lightering trade, a job where I can (perhaps) see myself spending the rest of my working days.

So why am I telling you all this? I know you did not pick up this book to read the memoirs of André L Le Goubin. I simply want to give you a flavour of where I have come from and why I am so concerned about mentoring. I know that your background will be different from mine, as we are all unique and follow individual career pathways. But I am also aware that we will have a lot in common, as you will have met many people along the way who have helped you get to where you are now, as I did.

These people may have been Masters, mates, chief engineers, superintendents, relatives, friends or complete strangers whom you didn't know and have never met again. The one thing they had in common was that they shared some knowledge with you that came from their experience and you benefitted as a result. They were your mentors. So what do I mean by that? Who or what, is a mentor? Let's just pause for a few minutes and look at some of the definitions of words I will be using throughout this book.

Mentor

The *Oxford English Dictionary* describes a mentor as 'an experienced and trusted advisor' and sources the origin of the word as 'from the name of Mentor, the adviser of the young Telemachus in Homer's *Odyssey*'. In the context of this book, I simply define it as the possessor and distributor of experiential knowledge.

Mentoring

One definition of mentoring is that it is a form of knowledge transfer based in part on altruism. I like this definition as, for me it sums up the unselfish act of knowledge transfer that I benefitted from in my early days at sea. For our purposes, I have followed this theme and defined mentoring as 'the act of sharing knowledge without a designated reward'. This definition in itself has caused a certain amount of debate, but I believe it suffices.

I have had lengthy discussions with various people about the definition of mentoring and whether there is actually a designated reward for mentoring. I do not believe that there is. However, many would disagree. This is exactly what I want! You will not agree with everything I say, I know that and, if you think there is a reward for mentoring then great, but I am currently holding fast with my belief.

I am open to discussion and, after finishing this book, I hope that you will engage with this conversation about mentoring and then tell me what you think. To help facilitate this, The Nautical Institute has set up an online mentoring forum and this can be found at www.nautinst.org/en/forums/mentoring/.

Experiential knowledge

I have defined this as knowledge gained from professional 'on the job' experiences and reflected upon. This knowledge can come from a wide variety of sources or experiences but, in my opinion, it often has the most impact when it comes from an accident, incident or near miss. However, it does need to be reflected upon before it can become experiential learning. I will say much more on this further into the book.

Candidate

I really struggled with this one as I would like to use the word apprentice, as traditionally that is what I think we are when receiving mentoring advice, but the word does not seem to be politically acceptable these days and is considered somewhat demeaning. Then I tried mentee, but that just doesn't sound right and so I finally settled on candidate. This term would also include a person at any stage of life because, as most of you I think would agree, learning never ceases. I simply define a candidate as anyone receiving experiential knowledge via mentoring.

Reflection

According to the Institute of Work Based Learning, reflection is 'a thoughtful (in the sense of deliberative) consideration of your experiences, which leads you to decide what the experience means to you'. Over the last few years, reflection has become a very useful tool for me, particularly to review the actions I have taken and to help me be comfortable with the decisions I have made. A little later in this book we will take another look at reflection from a practical mariner's point of view and tie this in to how, through reflection, we can be more successful mentors in today's merchant navy.

Just before we go on, however, I need to mention to you something about my views on race, religion and culture. Why? Because, in this book you will hear me talk a lot about language, culture and cultural differences as we discuss the barriers to mentoring – and I need you to understand my views as I don't want you to dismiss me as a racist or bigot. I am not. I have friends who are Catholic, Protestant, Hindu and Atheist and I also have friends whose religious beliefs I have no idea about. My elder sister is an ordained Minister and I have my own views on religion which I do not share unless asked.

You see personally, I don't care what colour your skin is, what language you speak or which God, if any, you worship, as we all share a common bond – and that is the sea. Whether you are a Master, manager, shipowner, operator, teacher, engineer or maritime lawyer, one thing I can pretty much guarantee is that we are connected in some way by the sea.

I love the sea. I was born near it and can't remember a time when I did not go fishing. Even now, although I work at sea, I also spend a lot of my spare time on, in, under or at least near the sea. When I die, I would like my ashes to be scattered in the Gulf Stream so that I will sail the North Atlantic on my final voyage. That's not morbid, it is just the person I am. I am white and speak English as my first language – I have friends who are not, and don't. It just does not matter, but it is very important to me that you understand this.

There is one last thing that I must point out before we move on to the basics of mentoring. Throughout this book you will read examples of accidents and incidents. These are not examples of actual accidents or incidents I have investigated, as it would not be appropriate for me to use those without the express permission of all the parties involved. The examples I have used are fictional but based on facts that I have acquired anecdotally, from reading through hundreds of published accident reports and from my own experiences. Unless I specifically say that the example is real, any similarity to cases I have attended is purely coincidental.

Chapter 1

The basics of mentoring

If you look back over my introduction you will see that I mention mentors a number of times and that it is clear how important they have been to me. There were the fishermen who put up with an eight year-old boy on their boat and passed on the knowledge that set me on my way. There was the knowledge that, in part, my grandfather had passed on because he was a full-time fisherman as well as a pilot. Finally there was the wisdom from the Master of the small cargo ship and his willingness to teach the fundamentals of seamanship to an adolescent boy, keen to learn. I still think about him most days, even although he crossed the bar many years ago.

Added to this were all the deepsea Masters, chief officers, second and third officers (and the engineers) who passed on so much to me in my formative years, together with my peers on the fast ferries and in the pilotage service who were so often willing to share knowledge. As I gained more experience so things changed somewhat. Not only was I gaining experiential knowledge from others, but I was now in a position to pass it on. Unknowingly at the time, I had crossed the line and become a mentor as well as a candidate.

Today I am constantly crossing that line as I gain experiential knowledge on the one hand and use every opportunity that arises to pass on my knowledge, on the other. Don't get me wrong, this is not a perfect system and I am reminded of a situation not so long ago when I sought advice, outside my scope of knowledge, only to be told by another (who had the information I needed) in no uncertain terms that he would not impart it. This is where the ability to reflect comes in.

I considered this reaction and determined why it had come about. Was it my approach or was there something far more serious as the underlying cause? Having determined the latter, I moved on, found another person capable and willing to share the knowledge, and so got to where I needed to be.

But what is a mentor? What qualifications are required? Mentors are not mythical creatures or cloaked professors; it is you or me, a Master, mate, chief engineer, second, bosun, superintendent or stranger – in fact anybody who will share a piece of knowledge or experience. Anyone can be a mentor and the sharing of knowledge transcends race, language, creed or any other difference we may share.

What I would like you to do now is take a few minutes out of your busy schedule and reflect holistically on your career to date and, in particular, how you have got to where you are now. Is there anyone that stands out as a mentor as I have described? I'll bet there is, and that you can remember their name and probably the occasion on which they passed certain vital pieces of experiential knowledge that have stayed with you throughout your professional career to date. If I am not mistaken, you will now be smiling as you fondly remember certain people and experiences in your past that have made an impression on you.

Let me share one of my moments with you. I was a mid-term deck cadet on board a product tanker transiting the Gibraltar Strait eastbound. It was the evening between 20.00-24.00 and the third officer on watch was on his first trip. The Master was on the bridge and, due to the large amount of traffic around, took the con. The Master was talking about teaching in colleges and how he would never make a good teacher as the three of us grouped around the radar. (We did not have ARPA yet and so we were hand-plotting with chinagraph pencil on the screen).

The Master asked me to pay close attention for crossing traffic both visually and on the radar and let him know if anything was coming. A little later he asked why I hadn't reported the ferry that had just left the African side. Simple: I hadn't seen it! There were too many background lights to pick it out visually, even when I knew it was there and there was nothing showing on the radar – or so I thought. Then the 'old man' as the Master is commonly known, showed me the piece of cliff that had 'detached' itself from the coast and was heading in our direction.

I have never forgotten that moment as I received that invaluable piece of experiential knowledge from a man 'who could never teach'. How important it was to become some 13 years later when I became Master of a cross-Channel ferry on the Dover Strait.

Now I want you to reverse the process and reflect on an occasion when you have been a mentor and passed on a piece of experiential knowledge. I wonder how easy this is for you – probably not as easy as when you reflected on those who had been a mentor to you. It is not uncommon for people to be unable to think of one occasion when they were a mentor, yet know that they are passing on experiential knowledge.

Don't worry too much about this, I have been studying the subject for years and still sometimes find it hard to think of specific occasions. Yet I frequently hear stories of people who have helped others on their way and the bond that this has formed between them, generally from the candidate, but not always. There must be so many other stories that exist where mentoring has taken place on an *ad hoc* basis and, although a bond may not have formed between the mentor and candidate, experiential knowledge was still transferred.

I had a lovely opportunity recently to pass something on. I was on board a ship at anchor in a small cut, off a river, where there was very little room either side or behind us, where a number of barges had moored.

On the advice of the pilot who had brought the vessel in, she was moored with only two shackles (on deck) on the port anchor, approximately 54 metres of anchor chain. While

I was on the bridge I noticed the wind had increased slightly and that we had started to drag anchor. The duty officer had not noticed this as he was monitoring the position using the Differential Global Positioning System (DGPS), rather than looking out of the bridge window.

I quietly pointed out that we were moving to the third officer and suggested he call the Master which, after a little persuasion, he did. They successfully moved the vessel back into position and re-anchored, this time with just a little more anchor cable. And there we remained for a considerable time. The third officer was obviously quite embarrassed by this and later in the day when I returned to the bridge, he came to me to explain what happened. It was his first trip as third officer and he thought the DGPS would tell him when they moved out of position. It took just five minutes for me to explain to him how to use visual transits to tell if they were moving, and I was glad to do so. And what pleased me even more was that I later saw him explaining it to one of the deck cadets.

Throughout this book you will find times when I get personal as I explain the concepts of mentoring and how mentors and mentoring have affected me. I make no apology for this as mentoring is personal; normally it is one-to-one between the mentor and the candidate. This is what sets mentoring apart from teaching or coaching. We are not paid for it and, in my opinion, there is no designated reward. Therefore, you have to want to be a mentor – or at least want to share your experience. And that is personal.

A little while back I defined what I mean by experiential knowledge as knowledge gained from professional 'on the job' experiences and reflected upon. But what do I really mean by this? Let me try to explain. Consider for a moment the worst experience you have ever had, perhaps a maritime incident, a death in your close family or any number of dreadful things that make up a normal life.

As you have reflected on that time, you will have gained a significant amount of knowledge, perhaps on what went wrong and how a similar incident can be avoided in the future. Or maybe you would consider how you feel about the loss of a loved one. This is experiential knowledge. There will come a time when you can share that awareness with someone else, to prevent a similar incident to yours, or perhaps to comfort someone. As you share this experiential knowledge, you will have made their life better.

This is what I mean when I say that experiences can be good or bad, but the knowledge that comes from those experiences can only ever be good. And do remember, it is the knowledge you need to share, not the actual experience that the knowledge came from, so don't feel that this is in any way a belittling or potentially embarrassing experience.

One of my old Masters used to often remind me that "The man who never made a mistake, never made anything else". I later found out that he had been involved in a tragic incident at sea where people were lost. He never spoke about it, but as I reflect on what he taught me I know that I benefitted from the experiential knowledge he gained from that incident.

We all know the old saying 'time heals all'. Well, I have come to realise that this does not happen overnight. A bad experience becomes useful knowledge after a time and so don't expect this experiential knowledge to happen immediately.

That is what this is all about. How to be a mentor and pass on experiential knowledge, or as one of my former consultant colleagues puts it, transferring "those gems of wisdom that are passed on during an operation, and that consolidate theoretical knowledge." Later in the book, I will challenge you to become a mentor and give you some ideas on how to undertake it in today's modern merchant navy. I look forward to your feedback. But first, as we are now in a reflective mood, let us look back at some of the history of mentoring.

I have no idea when mentoring actually started but would imagine that it came soon after the origins of mankind. Consider hunters gathered around a fire planning their next expedition. I can only assume that a substantial amount of experiential knowledge was shared by the elders with the younger hunters on how to capture the required animal. I can also imagine ancient tribes telling stories around a fire as a means of knowledge transfer before the days when they had the capability to write it down.

Think also about early navigators and how they found their way across the oceans, compared with the way we do it today. Knowledge must have been passed on by mentoring as the young midshipmen gained experience and progressed through the ranks to command, when the process began all over again.

Leading on from this, many old established organisations such as The Honourable Company of Master Mariners traditionally have a system of mentoring, so that knowledge can be shared.

I often wonder, as a father, am I also a mentor to my children? As I write this section I think of a recent trip when I was high up in the Rocky Mountains camping with my wife and two younger children. During that precious time, I was able to show my son how to stack up wood and start a campfire and how to tie a rolling hitch on the tent guy ropes so that they didn't slip. Does that make me a mentor or was I just being a Dad? Under my definition of a mentor, I was certainly passing on experiential knowledge which I had reflected upon. I began camping at an early age and often think of the fun we had as a crowd of youngsters under canvas. But then, is there a designated reward?

I had an interesting conversation recently with a Master significantly older than me. We were considering who we are and what effect we will have had on the world when we leave. His opinion was that we are what we leave behind, as that is how we are remembered. Of course, he was talking about his family. With this in mind I wonder then if being a parent precludes us from being a mentor to our children as the better we educate them in the skills of life, the better they do and we are remembered as the previous generation.

But what if you don't have children? Think back to my introduction and the Irish Master who taught me so much when I was a young boy on his vessel. He and his wife didn't have children. Just before his untimely death, I believe he told an acquaintance that I was the son that he never had. Yet that takes nothing away from my father who I was so very fond of – it just enriched my upbringing. I will leave it to you to decide.

Chapter 2
The value and importance of mentoring

This book on mentoring began life based on research I conducted in partnership with The Nautical Institute and Middlesex University in London for a Master of Arts degree – MA – which I gained in 2009. The purpose of my research was to show that if experiential knowledge was not transferred from senior to junior officers on board modern merchant navy vessels by mentoring this could be a contributory factor in marine accidents. I also wanted to identify the barriers that were preventing this transfer of knowledge and to provide practical suggestions to help re-establish the flow of knowledge.

In addition, it was (and still is) my aim to engage the maritime community in conversations about mentoring and the transfer of experiential knowledge. For, although a person may not agree with what I say, the very act of disagreeing is engaging and helps to raise the profile of the mentoring debate.

Through this research I was able more clearly to understand:

- Where the gaps in knowledge at sea are
- Causes of this knowledge gap
- Practical measures to re-establish the knowledge flow

Over the last few years I have developed this research and have investigated the many ways that companies, institutions and individuals transfer their experience to others and I am now in a position to pass my findings on.

Throughout this book you will see instances in which a Master, chief officer, chief engineer and others have commented about various issues relating to mentoring. Often these comments are taken directly from the research questionnaires I distributed and, while due to agreed confidentiality I can't name the responder, I gratefully acknowledge their contribution by engaging in this conversation.

But where did this all start? What really set me off on this was an article I read in a report from the UK's Confidential Hazardous Incident Reporting Programme (CHIRP) which mentioned mentoring as a factor in the incident. The report is available on the website www.chirp.co.uk and appeared in Issue 10 of CHIRP *Feedback*. I have selected some excerpts.

One of the company's ships had a near miss, as reported by the Master. The duty officer concerned was a properly certificated officer. He was the third mate carrying out the second mate's watch (12.00 to 16.00) as the Master had just sacked his second mate for incompetence and was sailing short-handed for one voyage. The Master had kept the 08.00 to 12.00 watch himself and handed over to the other officer at 12.00 but was still on the bridge.

Incident details

Time: 12:30 Ships time

Wx: Sea slight wind Force 3, visibility good

Location: Vessel approaching TSS

No navigational danger or ship within 5 nm on stbd side, other ship being tracked on radar since 11.45. ARPA indicated other ship crossing ahead of own ship TCPA 10 minutes, CPA 0.35 nm ahead. Master on bridge. Duty officer came and stood on steering position close to helmsman. Duty officer altered course to port. Other ship maintained course and speed. Own ship passed very close astern of other vessel (ARPA shows CPA as zero). There has been no communication with the other vessel, the VTS or with the Master who was standing on the bridge wing a few feet away.

Company comment: The action taken by the duty officer is a clear violation of Rules 15 & 17 of the Collision Regulations.

Rule 15 (crossing situation) - This makes own ship the stand-on vessel.

Rule 17 (action by stand-on vessel) - Own ship is required to hold her course and speed. A power-driven vessel which takes action to avoid collision 'shall, if the circumstances of the case admit, not alter course to port for a vessel on her port side'.

If the duty officer was concerned about the other vessel, he should have made efforts to contact her. He failed to express his concern to the Master who was standing close by and finally compounded the error by altering course to port in direct contravention of Rule 17 (c).

Even though the Master was on the bridge, the duty officer remains in charge of the vessel unless relieved.

However, duty officers are required to keep the Master advised of any navigational hazards or developing close quarter situations. If an officer does not seek the assistance of the Master standing close by when he feels there is a risk of collision, would this officer call the Master at night?

For some reason, it is a common practice among young officers to alter course to port when crossing and when moving head-on or near head-on as governed by Rule 14.

The report asked that the case be discussed with deck officers to ensure that they are fully aware of:

● The dangers in alterations of course to port when taking action in accordance with Rule 14 or Rule 17(c)

- Their obligation to call the Master whenever in doubt. The guiding principle should be 'if in doubt whether you are in doubt – call the Master'

The CHIRP Maritime Advisory Board considered the company's comments and added:

- The ARPA indicated the other vessel was passing ahead (even if closely) and there is a risk that this apparent accuracy may have had an impact on the judgement of the OOW and Master
- Guidance on acceptable passing distances in the company and/or Master's standing orders may have been of assistance
- The sound and light signals prescribed by Rule 33(d) should have been made. As a general rule VHF should not be used in collision avoidance
- At no time does a reduction in speed appear to have been considered as an option.

The Master was clearly experiencing some difficulties with the officer complement and could have used this as a training or mentoring opportunity instead of permitting it to develop as it did.

If the company identified that incorrect alterations to port are commonplace in the circumstances outlined, then it should consider taking steps to identify why this is the case and identify appropriate remedial measures, such as a fleet circular, backed up with additional assessment and training.

The acceptable action in this case would have been a large alteration of course to starboard in accordance with Rule 17(c) (a round turn) or a reduction in speed.

This article made me very angry when I read it, not so much for the actions of the watchkeeping officer that are inadmissible, but the way the Master dealt with the situation. He took the time to write to the company about the action but took no action to address why the officer performed in the way he did, and to put him right. Situations such as these are not uncommon and it is in dealing with them that experiential knowledge transfer through mentoring can be so valuable.

That set me off thinking about mentoring and, more specifically, how I would have dealt with the situation that afternoon. Could it have happened to me? I hope not, as I would be appalled to think that the duty officer could not talk to me, ask advice or discuss any matter. I would consider that I had personally failed if this happened. But it is not an uncommon situation in my experience. All too often I have Masters moaning to me about how bad their officers are and how little they know and yet when I meet these officers, and I set high standards, I don't find them bad. Often they are just frightened of the Master!

Imagine a bulk carrier, afloat for many years and the Master and chief officer do not talk civilly. They are of different nationalities and the chief officer is scared of the Master, who finds this situation enjoyable. Ashore there are often laws against this type of behaviour but at sea it is a very different matter and more common than most people ashore would imagine. Because he perceives the chief officer to be incompetent, the Master has taken over cargo operations and ordered that nothing is to take place without his permission or instruction.

Chapter 2
Mentoring at Sea

During the discharge of the valuable bulk cargo, ballasting is to take place but, unbeknown to the Master, the hold bilges are being pumped by the duty engineer and a connecting line blank had been removed to facilitate this. The ballast water floods straight back though the bilge line and into the hold bilge through the open valve destroying a significant amount of cargo.

So whose fault was this? The Master, of course, would claim it was nothing to do with him; it was the chief officer's fault as he was responsible for the cargo discharge and the junior engineer who removed the blank would leave the vessel in that port!

I will talk a lot more about language barriers in the context of mentoring in Chapter 6. However, I believe this is the greatest challenge we have to effective mentoring and the transfer of experiential knowledge. But not just in mentoring, I truly believe that this is one of the most significant problems that today's merchant navy has to face.

In my example there was clearly a lack of empathy between the Master and chief officer. Was it just a language barrier or was it something deeper? I cannot say for sure, but these are the challenges we are facing today at sea and they are the challenges that we have to overcome.

It is easy to reflect on the 'good old days' when we all spoke the same language on a vessel; when everyone understudied the ranks above and assisted those on their way up; and when we all met in the bar before dinner for a drink and inevitably to discuss the day's work. Those days are gone and they are not coming back any time soon – if ever!

Actually I often think about how much experiential knowledge was shared in the bar before dinner. Often, as a cadet or junior officer, I recall listening to the senior officers discussing a problem that had been experienced and the solution that had resolved it. Generally, I was not part of the conversation but now, as I think about it, as I listened, I was learning; I was receiving experiential knowledge. I believe I, like so many others at that time, gained a great deal from listening to these conversations. But consider for a moment if the senior officers had been speaking in a foreign language that I did not understand. I would have gained nothing.

When I am discussing this I am often asked if I am advocating putting bars back on ships. That would be totally unacceptable for many as a considerable number of vessels are 'dry' and have been for a very long time. Therefore a bar is not a solution for many of these vessels, but personally, I see nothing wrong with meeting for a beer and a chat before dinner, when the vessel is at sea and operational conditions allow.

Under the International Safety Management (ISM) Code there are rules for the consumption of alcohol and the penalties for being over the limit are generally severe. So, within those constraints, why not have a bar? The only condition I would lay down is that when you do meet, all conversations must be in a common language.

I am sure that there are now many people who are horrified by what I appear to be advocating but, if it helps, here's an example of how it can work. I was on board a heavy lift vessel some time ago with a mixed nationality crew. The vessel came to the US and in keeping with tradition had an arrival party in the bar. It was great fun, with everyone speaking in a common language and no alcohol whatsoever!

How important is mentoring? When I considered this question I remember the following MARS report published in *Seaway* a few years ago:

Attempted suicide MARS Report 200721

While coasting at the end of a trans-Pacific passage, a training module was planned for two deck cadets on the bridge after lunch. Only one cadet showed up and attempts to find the other proved futile. The crew was mustered and a search began. Some crew members reported that the missing cadet had been seen before lunch, heading out of the accommodation.

When an initial search failed to locate him, the ship was turned around and a track line search commenced. Urgency messages were transmitted on VHF channel 16, and were repeated at intervals of 15 minutes. The coastal authorities were also informed.

The weather then steadily turned worse, with heavy squally showers affecting visibility and raising a sea of around 3 metres. By nightfall, several vessels joined in the SAR operations. Finally, at around noon on the following day, one of the participating ships sighted the cadet, still apparently alive. With two other vessels standing by, she lowered a lifeboat to recover the cadet. Unfortunately, the lifeboat was unable to make much progress in the still heavy sea conditions. Observing this, one of the assisting ships manoeuvred to a better position upwind of the cadet and launched the leeside lifeboat.

The cadet was duly recovered and after initial first aid on board the rescuing ship, his condition was stabilised. The operation ended and all ships resumed their respective voyages. After arrival in port, the cadet was transferred back to his ship where investigations and interviews were held.

Root cause and contributory factors

The cadet apparently felt alienated and victimised, as a majority of the other crew members were of a different nationality. Due to severe homesickness, and perhaps a lack of proper counselling on board, the cadet decided to commit suicide by jumping overboard.

Lessons learned

Inter-personal relationships between crew members should be closely and unobtrusively monitored by senior officers.

Cases of bullying, alienation and depression should be quickly detected and the victim's grievances should be resolved fairly.

With assistance from the company and radio medical services, appropriate medication may be administered and a crew member suffering from depression kept off work and under continuous supervision, if appropriate.

Cadets and new entrants to the seafaring profession must be given particular attention.

Special care should be taken by companies and manning agents to ensure that every recruit is physically and mentally fit.

The MARS Editor noted: Seafarers may not be trained in psychology but many, with maturity, develop a feel for detecting and dealing with personal problems among their colleagues. Given the enclosed working environment on board ship, senior officers and ratings should interact openly with younger colleagues, with trainees in particular, playing the role of friend, trainer and mentor. The Master and senior officers should certainly show everyone that they are approachable, have a sympathetic ear and can come up with practical and acceptable solutions. Whenever conditions permit, a party or similar social get-together can provide a welcome break from set and stressful routines on board.

This is a sad report and raises all sorts of questions associated with today's merchant fleet; it also reminds me of the value of mentoring. Later on in this book we will look at some of the barriers that exist to prevent mentoring and the transfer of experiential knowledge and ways that these barriers can be overcome to help prevent tragic incidents from occurring, such as the one described above. If this cadet had someone trusted to turn to, he may not have felt the need to take such extreme action.

The combination of both these reports and my new experience as a consultant led me to think that something had happened in the merchant fleet. Staff were not trained in the way they used to be by handing down knowledge one to another. In the past people would train their successors and, in turn, understudy the people above them.

That is how my degree studies and ultimately this book, which is a product of those studies, began life. Following three years' hard work, fitting in my studies around my work and a very understanding family, I completed my degree course. I was now confident that I had established that in many cases, mentoring was not taking place as it used to on board merchant vessels and that this was contributing to accidents and incidents.

Perhaps more importantly, I had identified some of the barriers that stop mentoring and therefore I am in a position to make some suggestions on how to overcome those barriers and restart (or improve) the flow of knowledge. However, before we go on and look at some barriers to mentoring and how to get the flow of experiential knowledge going again, here is a scenario for everyone to think about, no matter what their position is in the maritime community.

A standard loaded vessel was at anchor in a fast flowing river. The starboard anchor was set with five shackles out of the total of 11 (about half the length of anchor chain). There was sufficient water beneath the vessel but the holding ground was not very good. However, the pilot advised, before disembarking, that everything would be OK as ships safely anchor at that position all the time.

The Master stayed on the bridge for a little while as he was nervous that his ship had not been left in a safe position, even though the pilot said it was OK. After a while the need to get on with his paperwork means he has to go to his office, leaving the watchkeeping officer with instructions to call him if the anchor starts dragging. Much to his horror, about 45 minutes later he is called to the bridge and advised that the anchor does not appear to be holding as, according to the GPS, they are moving. In your opinion what should the Master do?

A) Veer (let out) more cable on the starboard anchor

B) Let go the port anchor

C) Get the engineers to start the main engine, heave up the anchor and move the vessel to a safe position

D) Try to get a pilot on board

E) Call the office and ask for advice

I wonder what your answer was. Until a few years ago I would have expected everyone to answer A-D but now I would not be at all surprised to hear that the first action was E as, in my experience, this is what sometimes happens in the real world. Even when Masters know what to do, they often do not have the confidence to make the decision for themselves, but will only do the right thing if the decision is supported by the office. But what happens when the person answering the phone, often in a completely different time zone, does not have the experience to deal with a situation such as this? The result, in the worst case scenario, is that the vessel goes aground and a very expensive salvage operation is required to refloat it.

No doubt there are a number of you shaking your heads now and saying that would never happen to you. Great, but what are you doing to ensure that those coming after you know what to do in this situation?

What about if you are the person ashore? What do you tell the Master to do when he calls you at 03.00 hrs (your time) to ask you what to do? What about if you are a chief officer, second or third officer? Would you know what to do, and if not, how are you going to ensure you get the knowledge that you need to make the right decision when you are Master?

I know that many are thinking in the 'good old days' this did not happen. However, we can do nothing about the past (we can only learn from it) or for that matter the present; it is what it is. It is the future that we can do something about and we all have a part to play, no matter what our position, ashore or afloat. As we move through the book you will find some suggestions to ensure that this scenario does not happen on board your ship.

Chapter 3

The need for onboard mentors

I hope by now that I have convinced you of the need for mentoring but if not, read on and this section may help to highlight the benefits. According to current opinion, about three-quarters of our skill base is learnt from experience. It is this maritime skill pool that I believe is not being passed on in the way it used to be, by mentoring.

Consider for a moment the operation of a vessel as a whole and how much we have to learn to become successful operators of that vessel. Can we learn all this in a classroom? I don't think so, even with the highly sophisticated simulators available in today's education establishments. Much has still to be taught (or experienced) on board to supplement the foundation of knowledge obtained ashore.

But who is going to do this teaching, how and when? This is where we need on board mentors operating in an informal system of experiential knowledge transfer, to allow candidates to experience operating a vessel under the close supervision of an experienced person.

The safety and security of cadets and junior officers is paramount and a breakdown in monitoring can have tragic consequences as shown in the example in Chapter 2 when a cadet tried to take his own life. Monitoring does not need to be in a formal system. When I was at sea, the chief officer and second engineer traditionally took care of the cadets and ensured that their training and other needs were taken care of. Some were better at this than others but the cadets always had someone to turn to in time of need.

The nationality of the cadets may have changed today, but I do not believe that the needs of an 18 year-old away from home for the very first time are any different today from any time in the past. However, is the pastoral care and guidance that we used to enjoy still there if the person providing the care does not speak the same language or come from the same or a similar background?

Mentoring can have a significant effect on team building as it leads to confidence between individuals as they come to understand others' capabilities and needs. Mentoring is excellent at breaking down barriers between individuals, and this leads in turn to the cohesion of a stronger team.

As seafarers undertake knowledge transfer between ranks, they quickly develop a clearer understanding of the knowledge required to successfully fill the next position onboard a vessel. This leads to a far clearer picture of career progression. This may slow promotion a little but I do not believe that would be a bad thing as I am often told that manning agencies get one or two good reports about someone's performance, and they are fast-tracked for promotion – often beyond their capabilities. Conversely, some junior officers demand promotion after one or two contracts in a particular rank – or threatening to leave – regardless of whether the senior officers believe they are suitable.

One Master told me that promotions happen very quickly and that people do not have time to experience their knowledge or, in other words, to put their knowledge to practical use before they are moved one rung up the career ladder. I thought this was an interesting conceptualisation of the learning process where people are not in a rank long enough to 'experience their knowledge' or perhaps to expand their knowledge base sufficiently with experiential learning to move on to the next rank.

I am also told by current seafarers that many officers today are promoted quickly and, as a consequence, lack the foundation of a proper knowledge base and that the lack of skilled seafarers has resulted in a need to employ people who would previously have not been considered as being suitably experienced for a particular rank.

I believe that in addition to our present academic training scheme, we need a system of mentoring (on board) that allows candidates to gain sufficient experiential knowledge to move to the next rank successfully and confidently, working hand in hand with the academic and regulatory requirements.

Ultimately, I believe that successful mentoring and transferring of experiential knowledge leads to a reduction in accidents and incidents. We are regularly reminded that accidents develop from a chain of events and, to prevent an accident, we need to break that chain. Imagine that you have transferred that vital piece of knowledge that breaks the chain and prevents an accident. What better reward is there? Of course, you will probably never know, but that is one of the reasons that I define mentoring as being 'without designated reward.'

Chapter 4

Reflection for seafarers

Reflection: 'the action of the mind by which it is conscious of its own operations'
Chambers 20th Century Dictionary, New Ed. (1983)

Let me try to put into words what I consider reflection is and why it is so important in mentoring. When I began my research degree I couldn't readily understand the concept of reflection at all, although it was clearly considered important by the university and was obviously going to play a major role in my future studies. At the time, I was trying to describe my career to date and how I had been working at Masters degree level in my job as a marine consultant. I explained this difficulty to my professor and he suggested I imagine that I am sitting on the top of a hill, looking down on my career as if from a third party position. Suddenly it became clear to me as I could easily imagine that. I could explore my career to date from any angle and then understand what it means in terms of the knowledge I had gained.

I have to say (although the university probably wouldn't like to hear it) that this was one of the most useful things I gained from my studies and the concept of reflection is something I use most days. The following is a personal example of how useful reflection can be.

Soon after I had that discussion with my professor, I was engaged in a major project as a tow Master on a construction project. The object I had to tow was huge, box-shaped and it was a critical move with minimum under-keel clearance. The day came for the first object to be moved and it was floated up, having been purposely sat on the seabed for fitting out. But, when it came up it was over draught and there was insufficient under-keel clearance according to the procedures that had been designed. I was also acutely aware that the project, which had been significantly delayed already, was dependent on my moving this object. There was also a 20 knot wind blowing which was right on the procedural limit.

My head told me that there was insufficient water according to the procedures (which also put my certificate of competency on the line as the port authorities were watching closely), that this was the first object to be towed in a series, and the departure would be very slow, and that the tide, although still rising, would soon be falling. In all likelihood, I would end up aground.

My heart told a different story! I had become very close to this project and was working with a great crowd of multinational, professional people of which I was, at that time, the only mariner on the team. I so wanted to give it a go but eventually I decided to abort the departure. This caused a lot of bad feeling and I was accused of a number of things including that I had lost my nerve. It was very hard to make people understand the reasons that I had called it off as they were not mariners and didn't understand the complex issues of manoeuvring a very large object in extremely confined waters.

Once the dust had settled I had the chance to spend some time on my own and reflect on the decision I had made that afternoon. You see I am a bit of a worrier, I take my job very seriously and I care what people think and I was deeply troubled by this situation. I mentally sat on my hill and looked down on the project, my role in it and the decisions I had made. I looked at it from all angles and tested out scenarios – especially what would have happened if we had sailed.

Gradually I became (relatively) comfortable with the decision I had made. It was the right thing to do and to have sailed would have probably led to a disaster. Of course, I may have got away with it and then I would have been a hero but I think, in that instance, it was unlikely. There are some that still think I was wrong and I will never convince them, but with my new found skill of reflection, I do not need to try.

As you will understand, it certainly is not easy when you have to make decisions like that and especially when everyone is critical of you for doing it. However, the developed skill of reflection is a powerful tool for considering experiences and for gaining experiential knowledge. As I said some pages back experiential knowledge is knowledge gained from experience that has been reflected upon.

This skill now permeates every aspect of my life, both personal and professional. Any type of decision-making now requires a certain amount of reflection but this does not make me any less decisive; it just helps me make better decisions. Further, as I later reflect on decisions I have made, from all aspects, I can become comfortable with what I have chosen to do. If it was the wrong course of action, then I have gained the experiential knowledge to take a better course of action in the future.

It is interesting to note that reflection is taught in schools in the USA. A few years ago I would have perhaps been somewhat critical of this as a waste of time. How wrong I would have been! I believe that youngsters of today are far more comfortable with themselves and with their actions (certainly in the USA) than perhaps I was at their age. In my opinion this level of comfort comes in part from their ability to reflect on their actions and beliefs and that they can then act accordingly.

For me, one of the best times to reflect is at sunset and I always try to take a few minutes out as the sun goes down. Ever since I went to sea this has always been my favourite time of day. When at sea what I try to do, if the opportunity arises after my evening meal, is to grab a cup of coffee and a large piece of cheese and head out on deck. Ten minutes of peace and quiet like this makes a huge difference to the rest of the evening, especially if I have a heavy workload. On a long ocean crossing, I always liked it to get dark soon after dinner and we used to adjust the clocks accordingly when we could. This fits rather nicely with my concept of 'sunset reflection'.

But you don't have to be at sea, try it at home. For anyone who has visited Key West at the end of the Florida Keys you will know exactly what I mean as they take it to the ultimate degree and celebrate the sunset in a unique way every day!

Having introduced mentoring and reflection generally, I believe we are now in a position to get personal and find out what your greatest concerns are. Then we can develop a practical solution.

Chapter 5

The 10 minute challenge

This is something I would like everyone to undertake who believes they may be affected by the problem. Sit quietly for just 10 minutes and reflect on your greatest concerns, such as a lack of knowledge on your vessel or your own situation, but not about the industry as a whole. This could be simply one major concern, or be comprised of many. If many, perhaps it would be best to make a list, as 10 minutes for reflection can sometimes be hard to come by, and you don't want to have to begin the process again.

For me, as a Master, my list would start by asking if anyone is looking out of the bridge window, or is there total reliance on technology to keep a lookout. Having determined your greatest concern or concerns, do something about it. In my example, I would talk to my OOWs anecdotally, and by using examples of clear weather collisions that have happened recently on modern ships would illustrate why it is important to keep a visual lookout.

There are many places to find examples of clear weather collisions and near misses. Your flag state will probably have a website – certainly the UK's Maritime and Coastguard Agency (MCA) does, with links to the Marine Accident Investigation Branch (MAIB) where there is a wealth of information. I often go to The Nautical Institute website (www.nautinst.org) and hit the link to the MARS site. From there you can do a search using key words. This is a free resource.

As an example, just putting the word 'lookout' into the search engine brings up some good results. This is one from 2009.

Collision in TSS

MARS Report 200957
Official report; edited from MAIB accident flyer 5/2009

A general cargo vessel was on passage from the Thames estuary to Antwerp. She was crossing the NE traffic lane of the Dover Strait TSS when she was in collision with a bulk carrier which was heading NE in the Sandette deep water route. No lookout was posted on either bridge at the time of the collision. The vessels both had fully operational radars, fitted with automatic radar plotting aids (ARPA), although no radar targets had been acquired by either vessel before the collision. The general cargo vessel was the give-way vessel, but, on a clear, dark night with good visibility, neither vessel saw the other until moments before the collision. The watchkeeping officer on the bulk carrier, after seeing the other vessel very close to port, put the helm hard to starboard just before the collision occurred.

A fuel tank was breached on the general cargo vessel, causing pollution, while the damage to the bulk carrier, although less severe, took more than a week to repair on arrival at her next port.

Root cause and contributory factors

The lookouts on both vessels were allowed to leave the bridge in an area of high navigational risk. In the absence of a dedicated lookout, neither OOW made best use of the available navigational aids (radar, AIS) visually to maintain an effective appreciation of the traffic situation. The bulk carrier, despite having a draught of less than 6 metres, was using a deepwater route which is meant for vessels with a draught of 16 metres or more. Although neither Master was on the bridge, standing/night orders were not used to alert the watchkeepers to the risks they were likely to encounter during their bridge watch. There was no encouragement for the lookout to become an integral part of the bridge team of either vessel.

Lessons learned

Complacency continues to be a recurring safety issue in accidents investigated by the MAIB. Shipowners should recognise the risks posed by complacency and ensure that their vessels operate with effective bridge teams at all times. Masters should make best use of standing/night orders to set operational benchmarks and heighten bridge watchkeepers' awareness of risk when appropriate. Masters must lead by example. Ships' crews are unlikely to apply the high professional standards demanded if these are not observed by the officer in overall command. The use of designated lookouts is an essential requirement for safe navigation, but continues to be regarded as a low priority on some vessels. The use of navigational aids is not a substitute for maintaining a visual lookout.

I like this report as it addresses many of my concerns. As a realist, I understand that no matter what the rules say, the majority of companies do not require a dedicated lookout to be on the bridge at all times and therefore the responsibility lies with the watchkeeping officer. I do not say that this is right but just that this is what happens in today's merchant fleet and therefore that is what we have to work with. So I would use this report as an opening discussion with my watchkeepers on an individual basis, prompting a discussion around the idea that this is not what would happen on our ship, would it?

But then I would discuss a far more radical approach. Let me take you back to when I was third officer on a large, brand new, ro-ro/container vessel trading the North Atlantic in the mid-1980s. A Master joined whom I had previously sailed with as a second-trip cadet and whom I knew had some different ideas for his watchkeepers. Having settled in, he insisted that the radars be turned to standby when we were in open waters and, in his opinion, acceptably clear weather. Now, bear in mind that I was on a brand new ship, with all the latest technical equipment of that day and here was the Master telling me that we were not going to use it; I was horrified!

We followed his instructions and it really wasn't too bad except it meant that I had to look out of the window far more carefully than I was accustomed to. Therefore, this became my primary task as I was more used to a quick lookout and then reassurance from the radar display. When we did encounter traffic I had to take a series of compass bearings and ascertain whether risk of collision existed. Does that sound familiar to the answers we used to give in our oral examinations? And doesn't it say something about this in the rules? Or am I going back too far?

These days, I often think of that Master and what he taught me. He was certainly a mentor within my definition of the word although I don't suppose it occurred to him at the time, and it certainly didn't to me. In fact, at that time, I can remember promising myself that when I got to be Master I wasn't going to be like him! In some ways I am, and to me that is the whole essence of mentoring. I just hope by chance he may still be around and read this as I would like to say 'thank you'.

We all want to leave something behind, both personally and professionally and, as I reflect on the use of radars and how it affects the keeping of a lookout, I think of what he made me do and how it made me a better watchkeeper. Now I am able to pass that idea on and so it goes on.

One of my colleagues talks fondly of another Master who on sailing from the Panama Canal bound across the Pacific unplugged the GPS and took it down to his cabin, forcing his watchkeepers to use sextants. Once a day he would bring the GPS to the bridge and they could check their positions. This became a real competition to see who could get closest to the GPS position and I understand that there was much disappointment when the GPS was re-instated. However, the experiential knowledge was gained and I am sure confidence levels grew both within their own abilities and as a team of navigators.

I must make it clear that I am not advocating the turning of radars to standby or shutting off the GPS as a practice to be employed. The use of technology in navigation has come too far for that since those days. But what about conducting a drill to simulate the loss of the radars or even the whole global navigation satellite system (GNSS) for that matter? It would certainly constitute an interesting exercise.

This begs another question, closely linked to mentoring. What experiential knowledge should we be passing on, given the amount of time we have and the barriers to overcome? For example, should we be teaching youngsters to use a sextant in this day and age when we have at least two fully functional DGPS units on the bridge? That really is up to you and what you consider important and I am sure that this debate will go on for some time to come. I am also sure that celestial navigation will go the same way as semaphore and the morse code; it will become obsolete and I personally don't like the idea, but there it is.

I first held a sextant when I was 12 years-old and, once at sea as a cadet, quickly learned to take sights and navigate by the sun and stars. There is a great deal of satisfaction to be gained plotting the noon position having run up a sight of Venus on the meridian taken a couple of hours ago – a satisfaction I have never felt when putting a GPS position on the chart! To be perfectly honest, I have been on ships that don't even carry a sextant these days and they trade worldwide very successfully.

We are bombarding watchkeeping officers with more and more information to assimilate and digest rapidly during the course of their watch. Do we really want to inflict the time-consuming and old-fashioned art of navigation on them? Perhaps a better way, if you feel like me, and you can spare the time, is to grab a sextant and head out on the bridge wing and take a sight. Then just see if the OOWs are interested in what you are doing. If they are, you have developed a perfect opening for mentoring.

Another of my concerns is compliance with standing orders, especially for when the Master should be called. I often wonder how many Masters, who share these concerns with their standing orders, have taken the time to explain to their junior officers the relevance of these instructions, and the potential consequences of non-compliance, for both parties. Or is a signature of understanding sufficient because there is no time for more, or perhaps a fear that it could invoke a response?

You see it's all very well putting these instructions in place but are they going to be complied with by a younger generation which perhaps fails to understand their significance? Ten minutes is all it would take to discuss the standing orders with each of the watchkeeping officers and thereby ensure that they understand the orders and why they are so important.

I recently asked an engineering friend of mine (who works ashore) to undertake the 10 minute challenge and to tell me what his greatest concern is for those at sea. After he'd considered he said that one of his greatest concerns was how chief engineers take control following an accident or incident. After all, the chief engineer is the one everyone 'down below' turns to in an emergency. How chief engineers take control is, according to my friend, critical to successful resolution of emergencies.

If they scream and shout then this will be infectious and the incident may be made worse. However, if the chief engineer is calm and appears knowledgeable then this too will be catching. If each member of staff is delegated a task then everyone will be included in the resolution and if the chief engineer is open to suggestions, they may actually assist in finding the solution. However, what if the chief engineer does not have the knowledge?

A little later on you will find a whole chapter on this subject but, for now, I think that we can safely assume that a phone call will rapidly be made from the vessel to the technical department in the office. In my opinion, this is not an unreasonable action but it can only work if suitable technical staff is available to take that call. One way of dealing with this is to make sure that there is a crisis team available ashore to assist if needed, but that this team should not be used for day-to-day decision making.

You see, the chief engineer may only be calling because he feels he is obliged to (before making a decision) or because the ISM system requires it, or even just because he is looking for a little moral support!

If I was in a shore position and received a call such as this, one of the first questions I would ask is what do you want to do? The caller may be fully capable of taking care of the incident and is only looking for confirmation of, what is in fact, a very appropriate response. Competent chief engineers must be encouraged and supported please, as we must take away barriers that prevent them making a call for fear of being seen as incompetent. Ensuring that they always receive an appropriate response will go a long way to building a trusting relationship between ship and shore.

But what if it is you that is going to receive the call? Are you ready for it and do you have a system in place to give a supportive and appropriate response? It may be time for you to undertake my 10 minute challenge and determine what is the most likely subject you are going to be called about at 03.00 hours tomorrow morning. Having determined this, make sure that you have an answer and if you don't, find someone who does and build a network. Ten minutes is all it will take.

During the course of my work as a consultant, I was on board dynamic positioning (DP) vessels from time to time and, to understand the systems more effectively, I undertook both the basic and advanced DP operators (DPO) course at a Nautical Institute-approved facility. As many of you will know, operating in DP mode requires total reliance on the equipment and for many DPOs this is almost like a computer simulation.

Don't get me wrong, these are highly qualified and capable operators and I have a great respect for them especially when operating a large ship within a few metres from a structure, perhaps with divers in the water. But in this scenario it is very easy to forget to look out of the window (it can be frightening if you do!) and on one occasion I was told of a small ship in the lee of a large structure with a very strong wind blowing. If the DPOs had looked out of the window they could have seen the strong wind whipping up the waves, but the model the computer had built only accounted for a very light wind and, as they came out of the shelter of the structure, the vessel was blown away. No damage, and more importantly, no one hurt, but a good lesson in spatial awareness on one of the most modern ships.

In my opinion, this was brought about, in part, by lack of experiential knowledge. If the DPO had previously sailed on manually operated vessels he would have been experienced in looking out of the window at the environmental conditions and anticipated what effect they would have on his vessel. He had not, so relied totally on his instrumentation and sophisticated computer systems. But the failing also perhaps lies with the senior officer or Master, if they were of an older generation and had the required knowledge but had failed to pass this on to the junior officer. There is a different problem if senior officers do not have the required experiential knowledge and I will say much more about this later on.

Mentoring at Sea

I hope by now I have given you some ideas following on from my concerns. You will have your own which may, or may not, be similar to mine. Now that you have identified your concerns I would urge you to do something about them, one at a time. If nothing else, you may enjoy a better night's sleep having done so.

Chapter 6

Barriers to mentoring

Language barriers

As I have previously said, I believe that language barriers are a great hurdle that we have to overcome to reintroduce and encourage mentoring on today's merchant ships and something that should be addressed at the highest levels. Everyone is meant to be able to communicate in a common language, usually English, and this is a required standard on board a vessel. However, in my experience, this is not always the case and little is done to ensure that seafarers can communicate effectively with each other. This is probably the only critical industry where this occurs. Can you imagine an aeroplane where the captain could not talk to the first officer because they spoke a different language? Inconceivable! Yet I have been on board a vessel recently where the Master could not communicate properly with the chief officer and any instruction, if in any way unusual, had to be written down.

As I have undertaken an ethnographic style of research into this over the last few years, one thing I have come to realise is that the problem seems to be far more prevalent on vessels with two nationalities rather than those with many. In my opinion, this is due to the necessity to communicate in a common language on a multinational crewed ship. By comparison, when there are just two different nationalities on a vessel there is a tendency for each nationality to communicate in their mother tongue. Communication between the two different nationalities using the common language appears to happen only when necessary; in essence, depriving the vessel of any social communication between the nationalities. This can lead to all sorts of problems.

Consider for a moment that you are the third officer on an old style ship. You have just left port and are sailing through a narrow channel before heading out to sea. It is a fine morning and you are on station aft with an old tug attached and chuffing away as you manoeuvre. You are Asian, like the other officers and crew except for the Master, chief officer, chief and second engineer who are from somewhere in Europe, Greece you think. However, you can't be sure because the senior officers always speak to each other in their native language and only use English when speaking directly to you or one of your Asian colleagues.

In accordance with your normal practice for arrival and departure, the chief officer is on the fo'c'sle, the Master, junior third officer and chief engineer are on the bridge and the second engineer is in the engine control room. Suddenly you feel the vessel heel to starboard and a few minutes later see oil in the water. Then the vessel starts listing to port. There is a lot of shouting on the radio but you have no idea what they are saying as you don't understand the language.

Eventually you get through to the bridge and let them know that you can see oil in the water. The other third officer tells you that the ship has hit the bottom and is sinking. He is clearly very frightened but you notice that the ship is not listing any further so you think you are probably not sinking. Then you hear the emergency signal being sounded and go to your emergency muster station, so maybe you are.

A frightening situation and one that is certainly possible onboard today's ships. There is an emergency, the severity of which is compounded by the fact that the senior officers immediately begin talking in their native language on the radios, so no one else knows what is going on. Only commands are given in English and you can imagine the chaos.

To me this is so unnecessary. If all hands were conversant in the use of English and it was routine for everyone to speak a common language when in the presence of a non-native language speaker then many of the problems associated with a multinational complement would be resolved. In the event, my (very frightening) imaginary example above, was made a lot worse due to a commonly accepted practice onboard many of today's vessels – senior officers who routinely speak in their own language and continue this practice in an emergency.

I witnessed a good example of how it should be when I surveyed a well-found tanker of substantial years. The crew was made up of four or five different nationalities and I soon noticed that when I walked into a room where an unfamiliar language was being spoken the conversation immediately reverted to English. I thought this very respectful and appreciated it. Then I realised that this was not just for my benefit. It happened every time a non-native speaker walked in. It was just a policy on board which everyone adhered to and, I believe, this was reflected in the condition of the vessel and its operation, which were of the highest standard.

On another occasion I was on board a well-found smaller vessel with a mixed nationality crew including a West European Master and chief engineer and a second officer and deck cadet from Eastern Europe. I had an interesting discussion with the Master about mentoring and language. The Master admitted he had never really thought about language issues on board his vessel and always spoke Dutch to the other Dutch speakers. He used English when he needed to talk to the others or include them in a conversation. This is not an unusual situation in my experience. However, this Master had never considered the effect this was having on the non-Dutch members of the crew.

The Master said that he insisted that all officers eat in the mess room. I asked him what language was spoken there, and he replied that this depended on who was talking. Generally, he said, each nationality communicated with their own in their native language. To be honest, it was like watching a light come on when I started talking about social exclusion due to language and the need for respect for each other. Soon after this very amicable conversation we went down for lunch and I was delighted to see that the conversation was primarily in English, but nowhere near as delighted as the deck cadet who was included in the conversation for the first time, I believe. He just did not stop smiling, engaging and interacting at the table.

What a simple solution but what a difference it made, especially to that young man's life! All of a sudden he was part of the team and included, rather than shut out and sitting in silence. If this continues, and I have a feeling it may, there may be a good chance that he will stay at sea and progress through the ranks, with the experiential knowledge of what it is like to be excluded from conversation because he did not speak the same language.

Let me give you another example of when experiential knowledge was transferred by listening. This links to my 10 minute challenge described in the previous chapter. I was on board a ship chatting with an Eastern European Master about mentoring, the transfer of experience and what his greatest concerns were at sea these days. His great concern was the belief that some of his junior Indonesian officers were agreeing to pass other ships in contravention of the International Rules for Preventing Collisions at Sea (COLREGS) ie green-to-green when it should be red-to-red, for example.

Then, when he is called or he comes to the bridge (he had a repeater of the electronic chart display in his cabin) he may be confronted with a situation that he does not understand. Further, the junior officer found it difficult to clearly and quickly explain in English what he had done. The Master's first reaction was to comply with the COLREGS but this is not what has been agreed.

This same Master carries a book of examples of marine accidents which he started during his training in the former Soviet Union days. He showed me the example of a collision which occurred between two vessels, the *Admiral Nakhimov* and the *Pyotr Vasev* off Novorossiysk in 1986. This collision occurred primarily because of a radio communication agreeing a passing of the two vessels in contravention of the COLREGS. Hundreds of lives were lost.

Then the same Master spoke about when he was second officer and doing some paperwork on the bridge in which he became engrossed for about 10 minutes. When he looked up, the ship was little more than 2 miles from a white-hulled fishing boat and on a collision course.

This conversation, in English, took place on the bridge of the ship while at anchor. Throughout, I could clearly see the third officer was listening although he was not included. However, I think he was learning from it as he spoke English reasonably well. He would not have learned much if our conversation had been in Russian.

What was really frustrating for me was that this Master had all the qualities and tools to be a good mentor. He liked sharing his knowledge, as I saw when I observed him informally training the chief officer for command. He spoke good English and had even compiled the book of accidents to use as examples. Yet he was not sharing his knowledge with the junior officers as he should have been. It is not clear why, but possibly because of language barriers, cultural differences, or maybe just because he could not accept that these bright junior Indonesian officers were the future of the merchant navy. How much better they could be if the Master were to share his experiential knowledge with them.

It is interesting to note that it only took me a few minutes to research the *Admiral Nakhimov* and the *Pyotr Vasev* collision on the internet and confirm that it was indeed caused by radio agreement in contravention of the COLREGS. So when I say 10 minutes is all it will take to pass on a significant piece of experiential knowledge, I truly believe it. Although I will say that I found a video programme of the whole accident, including interviews with survivors, and I spent another 25 minutes watching that. This extra time is a luxury you may not be able to enjoy as part of your mentoring, but what about your watchkeeping officers? Watching this style of internet video is part of their way of life these days and it can make your mentoring far more real and appropriate. Perhaps you could download it to a USB drive next time you have internet access and use it as a mentoring tool.

Following on from this example, the next ship I was on was again well-found with a mix of East European senior officers and everyone one else from Asia. I spent well over a week on this one and got a great insight into how it was being run. Mentoring was clearly taking place between the Master and chief officer, with the latter on the bridge for arrival and departure stations and clearly understudying the Master. Mentoring was also taking place between the second officer, both third officers and the two deck cadets. What was very noticeable was that there was no mentoring taking place between the nationalities, yet they all spoke good English and communicated well between themselves when necessary, and socially with me at every opportunity.

What was sad, for me at least, was that only the East European officers ate in the officers' mess room while all others ate in the crew mess room. I gently broached this subject with the Captain, a most amicable man, and he said that it is what the Asian officers preferred, but I am not sure. I felt that there was a cultural divide that the Europeans were not prepared to cross, preferring to eat in their own way and speak their own language at the table. In their opinion, why should they change especially as some were nearing retirement?

But what will happen when the most senior officers retire? Is the chief officer, now Master, going to sit at the table alone, or with just the chief engineer as I have also seen fairly frequently? Or will integration take place? I can only pass on the experiential knowledge I have gained in this and ask you please to integrate socially, at least for what probably amounts to less than an hour a day, speak a common language at the table, and strictly enforce this, and then see what a difference it makes. I strongly believe that you will never go back.

I spoke recently with a Master about this particular issue but he had taken it one step further as he was Italian and loved the social occasion of eating. Once a week he used to provide a couple of bottles of wine at the table and everyone had a glass and relaxed when the operational conditions allowed, for instance, when they were at sea. All the chatter was in English which he said was a bit difficult at first but when people lost their embarrassment there was no problem.

Having accepted that language barriers exist, we need to consider what can be done to overcome those barriers. This book is primarily about mentoring but I do believe that many problems on board today's merchant fleet can be overcome by sorting out the language barriers.

I do understand that this is not an easy task. As one European Master of a specialist ship reminded me, it was often easier to do something himself than work out what words he needed in English and then have the officers translate from the English into their own language. This can constitute a serious problem. Consider a recent situation where I was working with an Asian Master and Chinese chief officer. Both were excellent seafarers but they struggled to communicate on anything that was out of the ordinary. When the Master needed something that was unusual he used to write down his instructions and communicate in that manner. I wonder what would have happened in an emergency.

The main advice that I can give on this is to practise at every opportunity where it is safe to do so. Yes, there will be times where you have to communicate in your own language to make sure that your instructions are fully understood, but try to limit these occasions as much as you can. Importantly, try to keep social communications in a common language. Of course, what you do in the sanctity of your cabin is entirely up to you!

Please insist that a common language that everyone understands is spoken in the mess room and be very strict about this. It will probably not be popular at first but in time I am sure that most will see the benefit and you will reap rewards. Think again of the example of the cadet on board the tug with the Dutch Master and the difference it made to him that day. He, like so many, is the future of our merchant marine and we need good people to take our place in the future, so let's start integrating everybody back into the team and not excluding them because of the language they speak.

Try to bring as many people as you can together socially as often as you can. The Dutch are very good at this and, as a pilot, I often went on board ships where there was a coffee table on the bridge and all the available officers used to meet there for coffee each morning and afternoon. This has to be in such a position that it is not a distraction to the navigation of the vessel, but that can be relatively easily arranged. Remember the common language so that the duty OOW can understand what is being said and share the experiential knowledge.

The same can be done in the engine control room when everyone meets for a drink or a cool off during the working day. Even if you can't discuss the technical issues of what is taking place you can chat socially. Traditional conversations among seafarers lend themselves so well to a common language, whatever your nationality!

If you are the Master, try to spend a few minutes with each of the watchkeeping officers each day. You will probably already spend a significant amount of time with the chief officer, but what about the other deck officers? I recall when I was second officer there was one Master who used to take his afternoon cup of tea on the bridge each day. He was such a nice guy and I learned a lot from him and, over time, got to know him quite well. I recall an instance when I had to call him out in the middle of my morning watch as I was suddenly surrounded by numerous white flashing lights which I could not identify. Tuna fishermen! However, I had no hesitation in calling him as I felt confident of his reaction. Are your officers confident of your reaction when they call you? Ten minutes a day is all it will take to ensure they are.

I often wonder if we can do anything from the shore to assist in this matter. As I have already said, I believe that onboard communication is one of the greatest problems confronting many vessels within the merchant navy and, as such, should demand reaction from the highest authority. This is not happening and it continues as an underlying problem, not easily identified as the root cause of an accident, but nonetheless causing social problems which ultimately can lead to incidents. Probably one of the best ways to help deal with this would be to raise awareness of the issue through informal education, and P & I Clubs can play a significant role in this from an influential but non-legal role.

Marine and engineering superintendents can also play a significant part as they regularly visit ships and are able to identify any communication breakdown on board. Care must be taken as often the superintendent is the same nationality as the senior officers so it is easy to become blinkered and believe that everything is fine when it is not.

Companies can become involved and use of a common language can be incorporated into the ISM system but I do not believe that this is the best answer. In my opinion, the ISM has had a significant positive effect on our industry but we need to be careful as there are so many instructions now on how to run our ships that we are at risk of removing the authority of the Master and senior officers to lead their staff.

In this case it is far better to educate the responsible people in the need for a common language to be spoken at every opportunity, gently facilitate this with guidance and informally verify that this is happening during ship visits by shore staff. If a problem is identified that can't be rectified in this informal manner then you can resort to more formal pressure through the ISM system.

On a positive note, I see more and more junior officers speaking good English and I am in no doubt that much of this comes from the significant amount of time they spend socially communicating on the internet. This can only help as long as the senior officers they are sailing with do their bit and communicate with them (and between each other when in hearing distance) in a common language.

It is not just between ship's staff that a common language needs to be spoken. Pilots generally speak reasonable English but almost exclusively speak in their own language to port control inspectors or local tugs, for example, excluding the Master and officers from understanding what is being said in the control and manoeuvring of their ships. Often when investigating an accident I asked the Master what instructions were given to the tugs and he did not know, as the language used was foreign to him.

Now I am not advocating insistence that all tugs crews, VTS operators and so on worldwide suddenly start communicating in English. However, when pilots give a command to a tug they should have the courtesy to explain quickly to the Master what they have just said. It will only take a few seconds each time and the Master will be more engaged in the procedure. It is also a good way for the Master to gain significant experiential knowledge on shiphandling.

I don't see a place for more legislation. The common language of the sea is traditionally English and I don't foresee that changing, but I do see a significant effect being made if we can introduce and manage change in attitude, which leads to a far better method of communication on board.

Demands on Masters' and senior officers' time

The thing I can hear you say is "all this mentoring business is all very well but how am I going to find time for it? I am so busy that I just don't have time to sit and teach the officers what they should already know." I am not suggesting you take the place of a college lecturer, but ask that you remember that it is experiential knowledge that I am asking you to share.

Remember in the beginning of this book I said this would take no more than 10 minutes of your time unless you want to take longer. That is the time it takes to drink a cup of coffee or smoke a cigarette and I do not accept that you can't give up that amount of time each day. Perhaps it would help to remember that each hour is made up of six 10 minute slots. Assuming that you are working 14 hours a day, then that is 84 slots. So I am only asking you to give up 1/84 of your working day!

As one Master described it to me: "Officers are struggling to keep their heads above the growing tide of responsibilities and the additional paperwork they face because of the additional requirements that have been introduced in the last decade. Masters also have a vital supervisory role of support of the OOW and this role is sometimes neglected because of the demands of the 'office' on the Master's time."

It concerns me when I see Masters sat at their desks in the office for in excess of 12 hours a day trying to keep up with the paperwork, especially at the month's end. Who is monitoring the duty officer on the bridge during this time? The simple answer is often nobody. Luckily, the ship's internet and communication system is often on the bridge or in the old radio room which forces the Master to go to the bridge and hence look out of the bridge window. But increasingly I see full internet communications in Masters' offices so they don't even have to do that.

I have also seen ECDIS displays appearing on Masters' desks so they can keep an eye on what is going on that way. But what happens when these Masters see something that concerns them on those displays? They rush to the bridge to find out what is going on. This may be the only contact they have had that day with their navigators and, during very busy times, it is conceivable that the navigators may only see Masters when there are concerned.

This situation is not your fault. It is the system we have allowed to develop, primarily with the advent of sophisticated communications, and I certainly don't have a radical answer to solve it. What I do ask is that at least once in each daylight watch, you take a break and stretch your legs by going up to the bridge to have a brief chat with the duty officer. Just reassuring them that you are around and available will have a significant effect; I do spend a lot of time talking to junior officers as well as senior ones and have come to understand some of their concerns as well!

In my mind I am certain that the senior officers on board today's ships are far busier than they were in, say, the 1980s when I was operating deep sea. At times I am both shocked and saddened to see the changes that have occurred to the merchant fleet, or more specifically to the mariners on board today's ships, as they struggle to comply with the everyday requirements of running a modern merchant vessel.

Let me give you a personal example. I remember not so long ago, just before I became a consultant, I was piloting on the River Thames, taking a 99-metre feeder container ship from Tilbury Lock to the North East Spit. She was a fairly new and well-found vessel, with a mixed nationality crew, including a European Master and sailing under a European flag. I was chatting with the Master while outbound and he was bemoaning the volume of work that he had to do in addition to his watchkeeping duties, as he was working six hours on, six off, with the mate. He told me that when the vessel was built, they provided him with an office, three decks below the bridge where he was expected to deal with the ship's business after his watch. He complained about this so they moved his office up to the bridge so he could complete his business in conjunction with keeping a safe navigational watch.

As we were coming into the Sea Reach clear of the tanker berths at Coryton the Master asked me if I was happy with everything on the bridge as he had to go into the engine room. I told him I was, but I, in turn, asked him why he was heading off into the engine room. "Oh, I'm the engineer as well," he said. It turned out that vessel was manned by just five people – Master, mate, bosun, wiper and AB/cook. I asked the Master what happened if he had to attend the engine room when on watch and he said that he would have to get the mate out. This vessel was legally but, in my opinion, inadequately manned. Going a step further, how could the mate learn anything from the Master and prepare himself for command, when they were both working back to back?

Fatigue

Much has been written about the effects of fatigue, and I think there is little doubt that fatigue is a primary cause of accidents. But consider also its impact on mentoring. How many of us, due to work commitments, have time for our own children? At times during a voyage we are often so tired that we can barely stand up, let alone take time out to show the third officer one more time how to carry out a relatively simple operation. Easier to do it yourself, do it properly and think to oneself that there is always tomorrow to show them again. However, that opportunity for knowledge transfer has passed and may not be recreated before an incident!

I would like to give you two short examples of fatigue that emphasise and underline what I am saying.

As a pilot, I boarded a small vessel heading into the Thames from Antwerp. After a standard Master/pilot exchange I took the conduct of the ship and the Master asked if I would like a cup of tea. When I said I would, he put the kettle on as he was the only person on the bridge other than me. He then sat down on a bench seat next to the kettle and immediately fell asleep. I woke him up some three hours later when we got to Tilbury Lock.

It turned out that he was six hours on, six off with the chief officer as there were only the two of them with navigational tickets, a common and (regrettably) legal situation. However, according to the Master, the mate would not do any of the pilotage and called him as soon as they closed the coast. The Master had expressed his grave concerns to the company but at that time no relief had been found. The Master was very apologetic and, I think, embarrassed to fall asleep in that manner but when I left, he did thank me for not waking him as that was the best sleep he had had in many days.

This man was so tired that he could not even stay awake when a pilot was on board. What chance was there of him teaching and mentoring the chief officer sufficiently that he could confidently keep his watch?

Just one more example of fatigue as I could go on and on but this one really frightened me. I inspected a relatively small passenger and car ferry running between a set of islands with only a maximum of four hours' steaming between ports. The Master and chief officer were six on, six off, and the vessel was well-found, flying a well known and respected flag. The Master was so concerned about the manning that he made no secret of the fact that one night he fell asleep standing up, leaning against the bulkhead and while on watch. Luckily for all on board, he had just made a cup of tea and when he fell asleep he spilt the tea down his leg which woke him up and he was able to make a course change, to avoid running into a reef!

Consider small vessels such as these. What chance is there of any mentoring taking place when the two deck officers are on alternating watches? Perhaps in the first example that was all the chief officer needed – someone to stand by him and give him confidence in his ability as they approached land – a scary prospect for him if he had just transferred from deep sea.

We have already established that fatigue is a serious issue on board merchant vessels and an undisputed cause of accidents and incidents. I do realise that most shipowners will not increase the staffing levels on board ships unless forced to by legislation. I would urge the responsible administrations to re-visit the issue of safe manning certificates in the context of not only operating the ship safely but also ensuring that the operator's workload is manageable, leaving sufficient time for other activities such as mentoring.

I would recommend that flag states abolish the watch-on, watch-off routine and ensure that there is sufficient crew on board to allow adequate rest. Isn't that what the hours of work regulations are for? In my opinion, there is no way that crew members can comply with the hours of rest laws when working six hours on, six off so they are having to 'flog the figures' to avoid infringement.

To be honest, everyone knows this, so isn't it about time that someone does something about it, or are we going to continue to see coasters running aground at 11.00 because the duty officer has fallen asleep in broad daylight. I do understand the commercial implications of my suggestions but every time there is an accident there is a huge financial, emotional, and often environmental, cost that has to be borne. Consider the number of ships in your region that have just two watchkeeping officers; what chance is there for one to understudy the other when they are working six hours on, six off?

I would like to see the Safe Manning Certificate become not only ship specific, but trade specific too. By that, I mean that the flag state looks at the route or trade that the vessel is engaged in when deciding the number of officers and crew required to safely staff the ship. Take a look again at my examples of fatigue. All these vessels were in compliance with their respective Safe Manning Certificates, but were they really safely manned? Once such vessels are appropriately manned, then it will be possible for mentoring to take place where generally it isn't now.

In this context I am pleased to report that some shipowners have considered this and have provided an extra officer on board their vessels to assist with the workload. On one tanker I visited, the Master had a young, newly qualified third officer to act as his secretary. This officer was also able to relieve another officer as necessary on the bridge or on deck. The system worked admirably and what wonderful experiential knowledge that young officer was gaining in preparation for when he became Master.

Another suggestion comes from Rik F van Hemmen in his paper *The Need for Additional Human Factors Considerations in Ship Operations* where he suggests that an additional officer be carried as an environmental officer. This additional seafarer could be a chief officer or second engineer nearing promotion and would deal with all the environmental requirements of the vessel while understudying the Master or chief engineer. I believe that this position would also lend itself well to the concept of mentoring and the transfer of experiential knowledge.

One chief officer commented to me that "Masters and other officers are so busy with paperwork that they have no time to observe the crew during their work. If I spend the day on deck when am I going to complete my other jobs, when am I going to sleep and what about STCW?"

This was an interesting comment, although I know that this responder was referring to hours of rest rather than when was he going to find the time to be a mentor. So what about STCW, mentoring and the transfer of experiential knowledge – are there any provisions for the inclusion of this concept?

I cannot find any reference to the knowledge sharing I refer to, but that does not come as a surprise. However, much is said about training and the minimum standards required for certification. Perhaps what we need is a structured training scheme, primarily for staff between cadet and Masters/chief engineers, which will take into account the necessary academic training and the gaining of experiential knowledge.

Notwithstanding the above, I know how tired everyone gets even on the best manned ships, so remember that nothing I have suggested in this book will take more than 10 minutes at a time, leaving, I believe, a little time to pass a little knowledge on if you incorporate mentoring into your daily life and routines. As one Master said to me: "There is just a lack of time for informal training. Undermanned ships and over-worked staff mean mentors can't take time out of their busy schedules or take a personal interest in the training of juniors.'"

However, you don't need to take time out to be a mentor if you incorporate it into your everyday duties. Let me give you an example of how this works.

You are the Master of a well-found ship with a good, sound chief officer who is keen to learn from you at every opportunity. You are approaching your discharge port and have been advised that you have to go to anchor before picking up the pilot so why not let the chief officer anchor the ship under your supervision?

If you do not feel that the company would support this, or if you are instructed otherwise, as so many companies do these days, I suggest that you develop and put in writing a proposed plan of your intentions. This could include:

- A brief statement that, in accordance with good maritime practice, you intend to introduce a knowledge-sharing system on board to help each officer undertake tasks in preparation for promotion
- You would need the company's support in this as it will be necessary, at times, for officers to be taken away from their usual operational positions
- Reassurance that this training will be undertaken under the direct control of the Master and will only take place when environmental and operational conditions permit
- Officers to be trained to undertake their new tasks by experienced officers before taking up any new position

Having obtained support and agreement in principle from the company, if that is necessary on board your vessel, discuss the plan with your officers and consider if they have the necessary skills to perform the task. For example, if you are going to ask the third or second officer to go forward to let go the anchor, have they ever done it before? You may actually be surprised to find that they have performed this task many times previously but didn't like to ask you if they could do it on your ship.

Let us assume that the third or second officer has not let the anchor go before so they need to be trained in the task. This is a job for the chief officer and next time you come into anchor you should send the two of them forward together and let the chief officer pass his knowledge on. Third or second officers will probably need to practise two or three times to gain the experience to do it on their own. This will require a little more effort on everyone's part so performing this training at 03.00 in the morning is not a good idea, but if the hour of the day is reasonable, I expect you won't get many complaints.

Now that you have another competent officer to let the anchor go, the chief officer can be released to understudy you, the Master, on the bridge and attempt to bring the vessel into anchor under your direct supervision. I am not going to tell you how to do this, that is up to you and your style will differ from mine.

I like to have three clear phases:

● Preparation
● Execution
● De-briefing

This sounds very formal but it really doesn't have to be. The second officer will have prepared a passage plan to the anchorage so you can use this as a basis. Let the chief officer study the available publications and determine the best approach and position for anchorage. Work together on this, especially if you have knowledge of the anchorage and can pass on any pertinent knowledge. This is not an examination or test of the chief officer's competency. It is simply providing an opportunity to pass knowledge on and letting the chief officer bring the vessel in while you are still there. Don't be surprised if the chief officer doesn't even know when or how to slow the ship down. As I said before, this may have only been undertaken once, in a simulator!

Then the big moment comes, and it may be a big moment for chief officers if this is the first time they have handled a vessel. It may also be a big moment for you if this is your first time letting someone else have a go.

Try to stay calm, which might not be easy. We do things naturally after a while, often because it feels right. That is the experiential knowledge we have gained in the past coming to the surface, but those new to the task won't have that experience so they will rely on you to step in if things are not going too well. Obviously it is better not to step in if at all possible and so again, feed experience and knowledge to the chief officer throughout the manoeuvre – the more the better as these learning opportunities may be few and far between. When to step in and take over is a matter for you alone.

Finally, with the vessel safely at anchor, take a few moments to de-brief the chief officer on what went well, what could have been better, what were the challenges experienced and how they were overcome. Keep it brief and meaningful and don't forget the officer who went forward and let go the anchor. It may have been a first for them as well. See how they felt and what was learned from the experience.

If you want to go really high tech it may be possible to use the VDR to record the approach into the anchorage and then review it later. This makes a great training aid and there is another benefit.

I have investigated a number of accidents where, in the course of the investigation, I have been provided with the VDR recording following the incident. I have to say that to date the majority of those recordings were not complete, as there were faults within the recording devices. In my opinion, these devices should be tested at least annually. The same ends could be achieved, if the system allows, by recording a training run and reviewing it. The chief officer may want to spend a significant amount of time reviewing it but you do not need to as the recording can be fast forwarded to the pertinent points. In fact, about 10 minutes should suffice!

Anchoring the ship is just one example of mentoring in action. Another good one is to let the chief officer pick up the pilot under your supervision. This gives good practice on slowing the ship down to a set speed and controlling the vessel to make a lee, often in the vicinity of a large amount of traffic. You have to be on the bridge anyway so it will not take up any more of your time. But don't only think of the chief officer? What about letting the second or third officer slow the ship down and, assuming that conditions are acceptable, allow them to turn the ship on to the required heading. Giving a young person the chance to handle a ship (under your close supervision) can have a profound effect.

Let me take you back to when I was about 15 years-old and a deck boy on that little coaster running between the islands of Sark and Guernsey. I learned to steer the ship when I was 12 years old, standing on an empty beer bottle crate because I was not tall enough to see into the binnacle. The berth in Sark is a finger jetty running north to south and affected by a relatively strong current which ran along its length, northbound on the flood tide.

By the time I was 15, I had grown tall enough to see the compass and the Master allowed me to do more and more of the approach until ultimately the day came when he let me berth the vessel. The approach to the berth was quite straightforward compared to the passage around the east coast of the island where we had to weave through numerous rocks. But once we had passed under the island lighthouse it was a fairly straight run in.

For me to be allowed to put the ship alongside the wind had to be light, a flood current running and the Master had to be able to light a cigarette as we passed beneath the lighthouse. In this way the conditions were judged to be acceptable and I was allowed to remain on the wheel until safely tied up. It still makes me a little emotional when I think of the amount that man was prepared to do to ensure that I gained (in his opinion) the necessary knowledge to take up a successful career at sea. I couldn't repay him enough and I never even had the opportunity to say thank you before he died. But I can try to mentor others as he mentored me.

The Master need not be the only mentor. What about encouraging the third officer to prepare a passage plan under the guidance of the second officer? Or allowing the second officer to prepare a cargo load (or discharge) plan under the guidance of the chief officer? Each of the senior two officers has to do this task as part of their regular routines so guiding someone else will not take up much more of their time (perhaps about 10 minutes). Traditionally, officers always understudied the next above to get to a position where they were competent and experienced enough to perform the function.

But this does need someone to set the whole concept in motion and once underway, hopefully it will become routine.

I hope that this section has given you a good idea of how to start mentoring and some suggestions of routine shipboard operations that lend themselves to mentoring without significantly increasing your workload.

Fear

Fear can be defined as 'an unpleasant emotion caused by the belief that someone or something is dangerous, likely to cause pain or a threat'. In this section I use the word to cover other instances when I could also use the words nerves, lack of confidence, self-consciousness, inferiority complex, loss of face, or embarrassment to describe the emotions that prevent the transfer of experiential knowledge by mentoring. For simplicity, I will stick to the word 'fear'.

Fear is a barrier to the transfer of experiential knowledge. Often the fear that we could be replaced inhibits mentoring. It is natural that a newly promoted officer will feel vulnerable, especially if sailing with an experienced and ambitious officer in the rank below. This will pass as you become more experienced and comfortable in your position. But what is this fear really about and is it rational?

I think much of this fear stems back to the massive changes which took place in the 1980s when many West European officers were replaced by East Europeans, Soviets or Asians; especially where the senior European officers remained on the ship and the junior officers were changed. This is a situation that is still common on today's ships, although I believe far more accepted as many of the 'original' junior officers are now in senior positions.

There is no doubt that there was a fear of being replaced and, to an extent those fears were well-founded, but as one door closed, another opened, and I believe that there are far more opportunities now than there were then. A quick look at the number of vacancies for marine pilots in Europe speaks volumes.

One place that I am told this fear can be acute is on board so-called mega yachts. This again is understandable as positions on these vessels are coveted and held onto firmly. But is this fear rational? Is a good and trusted Master in a secure position going to be replaced by an up-and-coming chief officer, for example, if the Master passes on experiential knowledge? I don't think so, as I am sure that mega yacht owners who employ good Masters will retain them. I also know that this is not always the same further down the ranks, especially if a manning agency is involved. Perhaps it is this competition that causes the fear which remains as the person achieves seniority.

I sometimes see people who are afraid on board today's ships. Generally the fear is felt by junior officers or crew members towards a senior officer and there is no doubt in my mind that this is a barrier to mentoring. I believe that it is possible to learn from someone you fear, such as a teacher or a coach, but I do not believe that you will gain experiential knowledge if mentored by someone you fear. It comes back to the trust which we discussed earlier. How can someone you do not trust be a mentor to you and, equally, how can someone mentor a person they do not trust?

In my experience if I go on board a ship and find people living in fear most of the time it is because one of the senior officers is a bully. Now that might sound a somewhat simplistic statement, but don't feel it is. There are some serious cases of bullying taking place at sea and ashore. These can result, at worst, in accidents or, at the very least, in an unpleasant working atmosphere. I know that some employment legislation has fancy words for this and set procedures on how to make a complaint and hopefully get it dealt with. However, if the bullies run satisfactory operations then usually no one is going to 'rock the boat' and get rid of them.

So what can you do if you are the subject of bullying and you need experiential knowledge? The only advice I can give is to reflect on the problem and try to determine why this is happening. Is it something that you are doing that is causing the problem? Are others experiencing the same difficulties as you? If they are, then it is unlikely to be a situation that you are causing.

Try to move on. Is there someone else who can give you the knowledge that you need? At least, if you are on a ship, then you will not be on board, together, forever. One of you will eventually pay off and, while it may seem an eternity to wait, it will pass and you can get on and get to where you want to be. Remember the experience when you get to a senior position and make sure that nobody ever feels the same way about you. That way you will have gained good experiential knowledge from a bad situation and others will benefit from it. Remember, experiences can be good or bad but the knowledge that comes from those experiences can only ever be good.

What if you are the one that others consider a bully and you are the one they fear? Is this a situation that you want and enjoy? If it is, then this is not a book for you, although I doubt you will have got this far anyway! But if not, then why do your staff fear you? I am speaking directly from my own experience here, as I have found myself in this situation and it was not one I enjoyed.

When on the ferries I was one of some seven Masters, each of us with our own ways, likes, dislikes, idiosyncrasies, etc. I believe I was certainly one of the stricter ones and, particularly when I was new, some of my crew members did not know how to take me. To overcome this, I tried to be absolutely consistent. What I said one day was the same as I said the day before and would be the same the next day. Gradually, my crew got to know exactly what I wanted and where they stood with me. I think most liked that.

As time went on, most of my crew became confident with me and were not backward in coming forward when they thought I was doing something wrong! To be perfectly honest, I could write another book on the fun we had carrying up to 2,000 passengers a day, in the height of the summer season, across the Dover Strait. I believe part of that was due to the fact that I drew a line and generally no one crossed it because if they did, they knew the consequences. But I also like to think that I was just one part of the team that we developed with everyone valued and contributing to the successful outcome of the operation.

Where to draw the line? Well, that is something that only you can decide and it comes with the experience of what works for you. You will make mistakes, as I did, but hopefully you will learn from them and be the better for it. Perhaps you have already drawn that line. If so, why not share the knowledge with your chief officer or second engineer, as I did, so when they are promoted they can rapidly begin to work well, helped in part by the experience that you took the time to pass on.

Rapid promotion

One of the barriers to the gaining of experiential knowledge often mentioned to me is rapid promotion, which seems to occur in regular cycles, reflecting the needs of our industry.

I have looked at the current foundation degree offered by the UK's MCA for the training of candidates for their first OOW Certificate and it looks very familiar. It is a three-year, five-phase course, very similar to the one I embarked upon in 1980, from which I achieved a Higher National Diploma (HND). Now new officers achieve an honours degree.

Further, the MCA reminds us: 'Master and officers need to know that the standards expected of the candidate (when competence is reached) is that of a person about to take up the job for which the award is made. Cadets are expected at the end of their training to be competent to start to undertake the job of watchkeeping officer, but they will clearly be lacking in experience' – MCA 2008. Nothing has changed there!

During my research, the respondents who referred to rapid promotion spoke of promotion between ranks and not the length of time that it takes seafarers to achieve their first watchkeeping qualification. This surprised me as many nations now only require their cadets to do 12 months sea time before taking their first certificate of competency. When I did my deck cadetship I had to have 24 months sea time before I could hold my Second Mate's Certificate. I often reflect on how much I knew half way through my cadetship and wonder if it would have been enough to be a competent watchkeeping officer.

Multinational and multicultural crews

This is always a difficult subject to approach and articulate but I believe that it does affect the transfer of experiential knowledge and therefore must be addressed in an ethical manner, supportive of the current regime.

As one former chief engineer described it, much of what happens today has its origins in the huge changes that took place in the industry in the early 1980s. Initially, shipowners continued to employ senior officers from traditional maritime nations together with junior officers and crew from newer seafarer supply nations. This resulted in an almost complete break in the flow of knowledge to seafarers as senior officers believed the junior officers could take their jobs.

This former chief engineer went on to comment that, with a diminishing number of experienced officers and seafarers, there has been a tendency for manning agencies to hire crews of several different nationalities. On individual ships this resulted in an almost complete breakdown in communication between crew members.

In some ways I am glad to say that the 1980s are well behind us and, in most cases, we have moved on from this sort of attitude. I spend a significant amount of my time on board merchant vessels crewed by a staff of mixed nationalities and, from my observations, I believe that many problems actually lie far more with language barriers than with cultural barriers. Even so, cultural barriers do exist and we must do all we can to break them down if we are to function as a cohesive team and to pass on experiential knowledge to each other.

We are all members of the maritime community so we share a common bond which I believe should supersede cultural barriers while on board ship. To achieve this, we need to have respect for each other and consider our actions, especially social ones. Are they acceptable to others or could they be considered offensive because they are so different? As mutual respect is developed and language barriers are broken down, then people may come to talk about their culture and beliefs in a non-aggressive fashion. This will develop a far better understanding of each other's culture which can be fascinating.

I realise that there are some cultures that cannot live together but in my experience they are few and far between and, if people make the effort, this can be overcome. If it can't, and real barriers exist on a ship, then drastic action may be required and one of the sides removed. However, who is going to take responsibility for this can become an issue as many companies rely solely on a manning agency to staff their ships.

There are many good and professional agencies out there which would deal with this problem but there are also some that are only interested in putting qualified staff in position to comply with regulations. If this is happening, then perhaps it is the ship superintendent or Designated Person Ashore (DPA) who needs to bring the issue to the attention of the shipowner. This is a book about mentoring, not the psychology of crewing ships. But they go hand-in-hand because conditions on board have to be right for a culture of mentoring to exist.

Chapter 7

Overcoming barriers to mentoring

In this chapter I want to discuss a number of ideas to promote mentoring and help develop the transfer of experiential knowledge. I have already suggested a number of solutions to the barriers that currently prevent the transfer but here I want to try to give a far broader spectrum of ideas so, no matter what your position in the maritime community, you will be able to help.

Structured training schemes

Until recently, I could find little indication that officers gaining their first certificate of competency were any less trained or experienced than they used to be. In fact, in some fields, such as the use of electronics, they are often experts! It is the next step or officers progressing through the ranks that is causing me concern.

For those seafarers aspiring to, or recently having taken up command, The Nautical Institute Command Diploma Scheme provides an open learning scheme based on the publication *The Nautical Institute on Command* with a diploma awarded to those who successfully complete, among other things, all the relevant tasks in a log book. But what about those officers who are between their first and last certificate? What is there for them to ensure they are gaining sufficient knowledge?

There are schemes available for this and I am aware of at least three shipping companies which incorporate them into their training and career development programmes but, in my experience, this is not common. I recommend that we develop and adopt a universal, formalised system of continuous professional development through the ranks – possibly by extending the Cadet Record Book system – this is a task book system – all the way up to chief officer/second engineer where it should meet up with The Nautical Institute scheme.

To do this from scratch would be a colossal undertaking but I believe that the structured schemes are already there and these could be adopted by a professional organisation which would develop them in a similar manner to say that of the DP certification which is administered by The Nautical Institute. While it is not mandatory for a DP officer to hold Nautical Institute DP certification, many oil majors, for example, require it as part of their vetting process.

Perhaps it is time that the same majors look at the training of officers between ranks and require certification to show that that officers have undertaken practical training in addition to their academic studies. Hopefully, they will also have acquired the necessary experiential knowledge to be successful and safe when promoted. I certainly know one shipping company that is looking closely at this at the time of writing and I am encouraged by this, but we need a universal scheme.

Successful completion of the training programme would then become a prerequisite before the officer was promoted. One Master suggested to me a check list system for officers to complete in the same way as sea time certificates are a way of ensuring the transfer of experiential knowledge.

The exercise I mentioned, such as second officers anchoring with chief officers having the con and chief officers picking up and dropping off pilots, could all be listed on a form. A certain number of exercises would need to be completed each voyage, each year, for promotion to be achieved. If this was written into the ISM Code then senior officers would be confident enough to allow junior officers to practise and learn from their experience and junior officers would be confident enough to ask for this training. This Master felt ships' personnel are 'programmed' not to think for themselves, as they are 'controlled' by the production of completed documents. If mentoring is to be delivered, it must be controlled by a similar system.

I like the idea of incorporating the training scheme into the ISM. I personally think that the ISM has been of overall benefit to the merchant navy and we are now so conditioned by it that we should incorporate a training scheme into it.

Often Masters take their written examinations well in advance of actual promotion and there is no refresher course involved. Academically I think this is acceptable but I would like to see, in addition to a structured training scheme of practical experiential knowledge, a mandatory testing of the level of that knowledge, before the assumption of command. This could equally apply to the promotion of chief engineers, other deck and engine room officers or any in positions of responsibility. If this were to happen, I believe it would strongly encourage mentoring on board ships as staff prepare themselves for promotion.

Social communication

As I have already discussed, consider for a moment how much experiential knowledge can be gained by just listening to people talking about a problem. If they are talking in a language you understand, all well and good. Conversely, if they are not, how much is lost?

In today's merchant navy, the onboard bar no longer exists and, with the way the industry has developed, particularly with the intolerance towards alcohol, I can't advocate them being re-instated. That will just not happen. What I can advocate is ensuring that ship's staff should still meet socially and discuss the day's events just as we used to, but in a language that everyone can understand. This may prove difficult at first but it is a problem that can be overcome if everyone adheres to the rules. A spin-off of this is that communication will improve throughout the vessel, making the operation of the ship far more efficient.

Meal times are an ideal opportunity to develop this social conversation. I feel it is necessary to reiterate this. All too often, I go on ships where the senior officers converse in their own language and the junior officers sit quietly or chat among themselves in their own. Neither has any idea what the other is saying and this is divisive at the least but can have serious consequences if it is the normal regime. It is also sad because so much can be shared between cultures with a common bond as we do as seafarers. But it requires effort, tolerance and ultimately, as communication takes place, understanding of the differences that exist.

So come on, please, let's have a common language spoken, at least at the meal table and if you find it makes a positive difference then expand the concept. It costs nothing to implement and you won't need the company's permission to give it a try.

Just another thought, what about arranging a film night? When I was working on deepsea ships, before the advent of the DVD, we used to get three reel-to-reel films per month supplied to the vessel and we all used to gather about once a week to watch one of the films. These days I notice that most people watch a DVD on their own laptop, in their own language and alone. Why not occasionally connect a laptop to a large TV screen and watch a common language DVD together?

On-the-job opportunity

I believe the merchant navy needs an adaptive, structured approach to mentoring but I do not wish to formalise the process. What I want is to encourage people to practise mentoring at every opportunity as part of the procedure, rather than as an addition to it.

Most established shipping companies had a formal system in place 10 or 20 years ago and in my early career it was expected that I would understudy the next rank above. This structured approach should permeate through all onboard activities and should be utilised through all stages including:

- Preparation – this could be as large as a job safety analysis, perhaps a 'toolbox' talk, or quite simply just the Master, chief officer, bosun or chief engineer taking a couple of minutes to explain what is expected to happen
- Execution – while the job or task is underway the mentor should try to point out to candidates important or interesting moments or better still, let them undertake the task under supervision
- De-briefing – after the job or task has been completed, time should be allowed for questions, comments or opinion

One can imagine the difference this might make to a keen young officer on the bridge, used to staying in the chart room plotting positions by GPS when approaching a port or anchorage and is now allowed to con the vessel, under supervision, through the stages. Even now, I still remember the pride I felt when as third officer I was allowed, under the Master's supervision, to keep the con of that large ro-ro/container vessel as we transited the busy Dover Strait.

I believe that everyone should be routinely training their successors. Even with small tasks not requiring formal preparation, every opportunity should be taken to pass on experiential knowledge. If this ethos is followed it should soon become embedded in the culture of the ship. There will be improvements in operational standards as a result.

External and internal learning facility

With access to the internet now available on many ships, it is possible to share far more information than ever before. Personally when I want to find some information, I 'Google it' as I am sure most people do – it is now a way of life. Throughout this book we talk about mentoring in today's modern merchant marine and therefore it must follow that the internet is going to be one of the greatest sources of experiential knowledge, especially if that knowledge is not available on board.

For example, companies could build websites to give mariners real time information on a variety of subjects relating to ships in their companies. This could include, for example:

- Ports visited, problems experienced and their solutions
- Discussions on cargos carried. This is a good way of sharing information within the company and of transferring experiential knowledge remotely. A good example is the carriage of nickel ore as there have recently been problems experienced with this cargo but it is difficult to find advice and solutions
- Accidents, incidents and near misses – lessons learned and useful information to be used for mentoring

Some companies have taken this a further and employ knowledge brokers, but there is no need to have such an elaborate system. I know of one company that used to have a radio conference call with all their ships (in range) each morning. What a great way of transferring experiential knowledge informally!

This concept could also be developed at an institutional level, with access to online mentors. I know from my research that there are many professional, experienced people willing to share their knowledge if we can just provide a means to make transfer of this knowledge easier. In Chapter 9, I will talk further about a new scheme that has just been set up to encourage this.

One Master came up with this suggestion. He pointed out that a more structured approach may be necessary on board. Junior officers could set down their questions, comments and areas of bewilderment at the actions taken in an electronic format which could then either be passed on to the senior officers on board or to specific mentors elsewhere. If sent off to a remote mentor some anonymity would be provided for the questioner, but if the ship's own senior officers were involved they could provide direct answers to the particular incident.

I have recently seen a similar scheme in place for safety issues. When a potentially unsafe act or occurrence takes place, it is dealt with immediately and a card is filled in detailing the instance. This card is reviewed at the next daily management meeting and any required action taken. The card becomes part of a closed loop system ensuring feedback. Perhaps this style of approach could be used to gain experiential knowledge from an action, when the heat of the moment has passed.

Distribution of accident investigations

I think that it is safe to say that we all like to read a good accident report. I know that when *Seaways* arrives each month the MARS reports are usually where I start reading. As I said right at the beginning experiential knowledge can come from a wide variety of sources or experiences but, in my opinion, it often has the most impact when it comes from an accident, incident or near miss. However, it does need to be reflected upon before it can become experiential learning.

Many countries' maritime administrations produce excellent reports but how many of them actually are sent to ships where they can be read and reflected upon by seafarers? One suggestion, which came from one of my former consultant colleagues, was to include a newsletter with lessons learned from incidents and accidents in the weekly Notice to Mariners that is sent to every ship. Not only would the seafarers read this but it would also provide an excellent source of discussion between mentors and candidates.

Just recently, the IMO adopted a Code to make marine accident investigations by flag and coastal states mandatory and these reports will be made available to the industry, so this is an ideal opportunity to ensure that they reach as wide a readership as possible.

In this context, thought must also be given to producing these reports in different languages as I believe so much value is lost if they are only in English. What use is an accident report highlighting the dangers of, for instance, operating a winch if the winch operator only speaks Chinese? Here, I believe, P&I Clubs already play a role but this could be increased significantly to the mutual benefit of everyone, by helping to ensure that the experiential knowledge is transferred in an appropriate language.

Increase in staff

I talked about the issue of fatigue in Chapter 6 and gave three examples of extreme fatigue from the many that I have come across. Mentoring was clearly not taking place on those ships for obvious reasons and the only way it could, would be an increase in ship staff. So how do we go about getting this to happen?

Perhaps all your company needs is for you to point out to management the benefits of increasing staff and the value this could have to ship operators. No don't laugh – it could happen! Failing this, we need to talk to people in the right places as I believe that it will take mandatory directives to effect change.

From any disaster there comes a lot of hurt, shame and anguish, but there should also be a good outcome. Experience can be good or bad but the knowledge that comes from the experience can only ever be good, subject to the changes that take place following the event. For example:

- The sinking of the *Titanic* gave us adequate lifeboats for all passengers and the creation of the International Ice Patrol
- The capsize of the *Herald of Free Enterprise* gave rise to the ISM Code and corporate responsibility
- The *Braer* and Lord Donaldson's subsequent report led to government-funded emergency tugs being strategically placed around the UK coast (although sadly these have now been disbanded due to government cuts). It also led to the creation of the post of Secretary of State's Representative for Maritime Salvage and Intervention (SOSREP) to provide a single point of contact with the powers to make orders in the best interests of the maritime community as a whole. A concept that many are now copying
- The *Exxon Valdez* resulted in the development of OPA 90

What I find really frustrating is why we have to wait for a disaster before we make changes when so many professional people continually draw attention to the various problems that beset today's merchant fleet. If you are reading this and in a position to help, please consider doing something about it before the next disaster occurs. Not only will you be facilitating mentoring, you may well be saving lives!

Chapter 8

Experiential knowledge through mentoring

Are colleges any different from those of 30 years ago when I first attended a maritime training institution? They have certainly modernised their teaching methods and have far greater access to technology. Simulators are so realistic these days that it is hard to tell that you are not on a real ship, making it easy to engage in an exercise, which is the way it should be. But I think the basic, fundamental knowledge that colleges impart to young people is much the same as it always has been, and is sufficient for them to go on to be competent officers, if they also receive onboard training to complement their academic studies.

What has changed in many countries is the length of time cadets stay in college before going to sea for the first time and the amount of sea time required before they gain their first certificate of competency. As an example, I met a Chinese third officer recently who was sailing on his first trip as a watchkeeping officer. He had spent four years at college before stepping on a ship. Then, he had to complete one year's sea time before becoming licensed.

To do this he sailed continuously on the sister ship to the one he was on when I met him for exactly one year. He may have been lucky and gained much experiential knowledge from the Master and officers he sailed with during that year, but in my opinion he lacked the depth and breadth of experience he would have gained by sailing on a number of vessels, each with their different officers and crew.

I can only compare this with my own experience as described at the beginning of the book. I sailed on six different vessels during my required two years sea time, excluding my time on the smaller vessels before I left school. Of course, I was lucky to serve in a company with such a diverse fleet, but notwithstanding that, I was at college with many cadets who had only served on tankers, for example. It was not so much the variety of ships but the opportunity to sail with other officers and crews who can pass on their vital experiential knowledge.

I have mentioned simulators and think they are an excellent way of gaining experiential knowledge quickly and cost-effectively for companies and candidates. I mention anchoring often through this book as one of the fundamental knowledge gaps that some new Masters have. If, as a company manager, you are concerned that this is a problem on your ships, then why not arrange for your new Masters to attend a simulator and gain that experiential knowledge before the incident.

Once they have the required knowledge, they can pass it on to their chief officers by mentoring through a supported company scheme, and so it goes on. The problem is addressed and resolved. I know that sounds simple but so it is. The simulators exist and they are not that expensive, certainly compared with the cost of an incident. Owners, perhaps you should consider for one moment, what is the insurance deductible on board just one of your ships? Now compare that with how many Masters you can put through a training course on a simulator for the same amount. I'll bet you will be surprised how many Masters that is.

Think about the effect an incident will have on the vetting of the ship, especially if you are a tanker owner. Perhaps it is time for those in a position to effect change to look at incorporating more of these simulated training schemes into a Master's certification under STCW. I do not mean when the written exams are taken, but at a point just before assuming command. This suggestion is a fundamental move away from the traditional system, but I believe it is time for that. Not only should Masters prove they hold the necessary certification but also that they have gained the necessary experiential knowledge for command. This leads back to the completion of a training scheme as discussed in Chapter 7.

What about teaching mentoring in maritime training establishments? I certainly think that the concept should be addressed and cadets should be introduced to mentoring, what experiential knowledge is, how it complements the academic knowledge they have gained and how it can be best gained from those on board. Whether this proves to be a difficult subject to articulate remains to be seen and is very much dependent on the attitude of the teacher toward mentoring. At least one training establishment has devised a mentoring module which the company it serves plans to make compulsory.

I believe there are many former seafarers in this world just waiting for the opportunity to come into a college and teach this subject. This would be an ideal opportunity to share their experience with cadets in a formal and structured manner and would give the cadets an opportunity to discuss life at sea, something they may not have been able to do before. I say formal and structured as this is not an opportunity for some old salt to come in and talk about the good old days.

This has to feel real for cadets and the former seafarers have to teach mentoring in a way that fits in with current life on board our merchant ships. Of course that does not mean that it can't be an old salt doing the teaching! This would also be a good opportunity to help cadets understand what they need to do to get the best out of their mentors and, from their point of view, what makes a good candidate.

This issue of what makes a good candidate for mentoring is a discussion I often have on board ships, usually with senior officers. I consider it usually comes down to the candidate's attitude, particularly how they approach their work.

● Are they willing to learn?
● Do they do that bit extra, helping out even if their watch has finished?

- When they make a mistake, do they accept that they are wrong, learn from the mistake and move on?
- Do they enjoy life at sea and is it more than just a job to them?

The list goes on but I think you know what I mean. A keen candidate can be a joy to sail with, especially if they have a sense of humour. As one Master said to me: "If people came to sea because they wanted to be at sea (romantic seafarers shall we say), instead of simply coming to sea for the money (economic seafarers), we might be able to inculcate them with the skills and knowledge they should have. Mentoring seems to work. I have had the occasional keen cadet or ordinary seaman who has been willing to learn. They appear to respond well when taken under my wing for one-on-one training and teaching."

I am not so sure there are so many 'romantic seafarers' these days and I am sure that for most money is a very important subject, but I certainly recognise the type of seafarer this Master described. Why do young people who grow up hundreds, maybe thousands, of miles from the sea head off for a maritime career as soon as they are old enough? There must be a certain amount of 'romance' involved but, on the downside, how many of those 'romantic seafarers' remain at sea? In the real world that we live in today, I really don't think we can call going to sea 'romantic'.

I believe that I was a 'romantic' seafarer. I still remember the excitement of seeing the Statue of Liberty for the first time or the Sydney Opera House and, probably one of the most beautiful sights, arriving in Tahiti at sunset and watching the sun go down behind the island after a slow Pacific crossing from Panama– awesome!

But then imagine today's young seafarers doing much the same and feeling the same emotions as I did, only to be told that they can't go ashore as they are considered a terrorist threat, because of where they come from, or because of a stamp in their passport. 'Romantic' – I don't think so. I know that this is a book about mentoring but this is not so far removed, as seafarers are often so disillusioned by the way they are treated in foreign countries and an atmosphere of disillusionment is not conducive to good relationships and mentoring.

One place that I often see mentoring taking place and get to discuss the qualities of a 'good' candidate is on board US tugs. Before we go on, I feel the need to make a confession. Before I emigrated to the US, I had a very jaundiced view of the country's system for licensing tug operators. How could a person who only had a 200 ton licence be allowed to operate an integrated tug barge unit (ITBU) that was often almost the same size as the ship I was on when we had to have an unlimited licence to do the same?

Well how wrong was I, and I am big enough to admit it! The US inland waterways and near coastal areas are full of highly experienced, competent shiphandlers who undertake an extremely difficult job with very limited assistance. These people often grow up on the rivers and knowledge is passed down in the traditional manner by mentoring. There is much that we can learn (and I have done so) from these professional seafarers, especially about the transfer of experiential knowledge.

In my mind there is no doubt that learning is a lifelong experience and I like to learn. I enjoy being a mentor but I also enjoy being a candidate. Let me give you an example. When I moved to Texas the proximity of the massive offshore industry in the Gulf of Mexico meant I became closely involved with DP vessels. It soon became clear that I would need a far greater understanding of the systems, so I signed up for a Nautical Institute-approved training course.

Just before I did the course I was on board a big DP crane barge in the Gulf of Mexico as the marine warranty surveyor for a tow to the Middle East. The Master of the barge was a very experienced DPO with a natural ability to be a mentor when he found the right candidate. In conversation he found out I was planning to take the DP course so, without prompting, asked me if I would like him to show me how all the DP systems worked on the barge.

To be honest, although I subsequently attended a very good DP course, I am not sure whether I learned more on the course or on board the barge. I have since completed the DP advanced course and my knowledge has increased, but I will always be grateful to that Barge Master for providing me with such a strong foundation to build on.

Do you have cadets on board your ship? When I was a cadet I sailed with a Master who took a great interest in teaching cadets and putting them in a position, as often as possible, where they experienced the responsibility of being a watchkeeping officer. One thing he was very keen on was making sure that cadets learned the COLREGS. Every Saturday morning, I was expected to attend his office with another deck cadet to recite the next three rules in our cadet record book. If satisfied, he would sign off on them with hearty congratulations and task us with the next three for the following week. All this probably took just 10 minutes of his time each week for each cadet, yet what a difference it made to me when I sat the oral examination for my first certificate of competency and to the confidence I had when it came to 'the rules'.

The mentor and candidate relationship

In our industry (and in many others) we now often refer to short-term relationships between individuals or groups when describing the interaction between professional people in the course of their employment. The Master/pilot relationship is one that immediately springs to mind, especially following an accident when I investigate how the Master and pilot interacted before the incident.

The mentor and candidate relationship can be very similar because it too can be short-term. It does not have to be a long-term and well-developed relationship although, when successful, it can easily turn into one.

However, for a successful relationship there have to be a certain number of components. There needs to be a common language. This does not mean proficiency. I have successfully been a mentor to Chinese officers. I speak no Chinese but if they speak a limited amount of English then we can communicate. It just takes a bit of patience and sometimes some dramatic diagram drawing, but we can get there.

There has to be a desire to carry out mentoring and this is two-sided. A mentor has to want to pass on experiential knowledge and a candidate has to want to receive it. This is one of the things that differentiates mentoring from coaching or teaching (remember my definition of mentoring being without designated reward).

There has to be a need for mentoring, as without that need it is unlikely that a relationship will develop because the mentor will slip into the role of a teacher, losing that desire that we mentioned before.

Trust is, in my opinion, an absolutely essential component of the development of the mentor and candidate relationship and needs to be discussed in greater depth than the other elements. However, please remember I am not a psychiatrist; nor am I trying to conduct an in-depth analysis of relationships. I am just a simple seafarer trying to get mentoring going again in today's merchant fleet!

Trust

I think as seafarers or members of the maritime community, most of us tend naturally to trust people until we are given reason not to. In some instances we have to. Consider for a moment pilots coming on board ships. We have to trust them straight away as they will generally take the navigational conduct of the vessel as soon as they walk on to the bridge.

I realised this early on in my career as a pilot when I boarded the second ship I had piloted after qualifying. I climbed on board at 03.45 hours on a wet morning in November off Ramsgate, UK, with 45 knots of wind blowing. It was clear as soon as I got on the bridge that they had had a horrible night and were clearly pleased to see me.

The chief officer was on watch, on a two-watch ship, and he told me of the very difficult approach to the pilot station and added: "everything will be OK now the pilot is on board". I certainly didn't have the heart to tell him how I was feeling as a newly qualified pilot, but just got on with the job and pretended I had been doing it for years. Everything went fine and we safely berthed but I certainly learned something from that experience.

So why do I consider trust to be so important? It is connected to the relationship between mentor and candidate that I have described because, without trust, I do not believe a relationship can develop sufficiently to enable mentoring to take place. Trust can come immediately, such as in the case of the pilot relationship I described, or it can develop over time as trust grows between people.

We talked about language barriers that prevent mentoring and now we will consider trust as a barrier to mentoring. You cannot pass on experiential knowledge to someone you don't trust. But how to develop trust? If this has described your situation then it is time for another 10 minute challenge. Spend 10 minutes reflecting on why you don't trust someone; what is it that they do that leads you to this conclusion? Now do something about it if you can.

Perhaps you are the candidate wanting to learn but feel your potential mentor does not trust you. I offer the same solution as for the mentor, 10 minutes of reflection during which you try to determine why you have these feelings and why you think this situation has developed. Each situation is unique so I can only offer general advice, based on my own experience and observations.

- Look at your role, are you doing your best or just enough to keep everyone off your back?
- Do you engage as part of the team working with everyone for a successful outcome?
- Do you ask questions when you are unsure or just 'wing it', take a chance, hoping everything will turn out OK?
- Do you use the expression "that's not my job"?

I know that these attitudes and many more can lead to lack of trust. I also know that it is very hard to determine that in some instances it is you who is doing something wrong and hence not getting the knowledge that you need. Believe me, the signs will be there if it is the case; you just need to reflect in order to see them. It may be simply that the mentor has had bad experiences before and now can't see a potential candidate.

One Master described his thoughts on this to me. He considered that modern seafarers lack a 'feel' for the sea. They don't understand the effect their actions might have. Cocooned in a closed wheelhouse there is little appreciation for what is happening around them. They may no longer keep a watchful eye on what the crew are doing, for instance, to check they are working safely. Weather can build up but they show no interest in changes to the ship's motion. A simple glance over the main deck shows water or spray coming on board but there is no understanding of the significance of this, or even why this should be recorded in the log book.

But not all modern seafarers are like the ones that Master encountered. If you are a keen young officer it is up to you to gain the experience you need and to convince Masters, such as my friend above, that with their help you can develop a 'feel for the sea'. If the Master tells you the sea is building up and asks you if you have recorded this and you reply "No", follow this up by asking the Master if he would like you to record it.

This may just lead the Master on to explain how important it is to record such events so that there is a good record available if a claim is made by charterers against the vessel in the future. A simple "thank you" and "I will remember that for the future" may take you a long way down the road toward more mentoring experiences.

Another Master observed that he felt that maritime training schools these days teach some form of navigation, but they do not teach seamanship. I would argue with this as, in my opinion, it is not for colleges to teach seamanship. That is the job of onboard trainers and mentors. This of course depends on how you define seamanship. I remember discussing this with one Master when I was a third officer. I had been on the same ship for more than three years and was heading to college to do my chief officer and Master examinations. Rather than come back to the same ship, I felt it was time for a change. The Master wanted me to return to his ship and asked why I did not plan to. I replied that I wanted to learn more seamanship on different types of ships. "André," he said, "seamanship is 90% common sense and you don't need to go on a different ship to learn that". I can remember exactly where we were when he said that to me, on the port bridge wing of the vessel, having just passed through the Zanfleet lock in Antwerp and that was in 1987!

Why do I still remember this? I'm not entirely sure, but perhaps because it was one of those gems of wisdom that he passed to me. Perhaps it was then that I realised what it was all about, and who would have thought that just a couple of years later I would take command of my own ship? How lucky I was to have mentors like that.

This is the crux of what I am trying to say in this book. This is where perhaps we have lost the plot, to use a popular current phrase. You see, I think the common sense he was talking about was actually experiential knowledge, although in those days I don't think the expression had been invented and he was saying that to gain experiential knowledge, it didn't matter what ship you were on.

So if you are in college and are about to head off to sea for the first time, don't worry too much about what type of ship you are going on; think more about how you are going to gain the experiential knowledge of seamanship, common sense, or whatever you want to call it, sufficient to become a successful watchkeeping officer.

Chapter 9

Shore support for onboard mentoring

From what I have written so far it is clear to me that we need to reintroduce mentoring at sea on many ships where it is non-existent, or at best very limited. However, there is much that can be done by those ashore to encourage mentoring. Take a look at the main directives in your ISM that detail the procedures to be followed on board your ships. Do those procedures allow for mentoring or do they, for example, require the chief officer to be forward for anchoring and mooring stations, rather than on the bridge understudying the Master? A small, but carefully considered change can make a significant difference.

It may be better to take one step back and discuss the concept of mentoring with the ship's staff and how they would like to proceed. This will probably highlight many of the concerns, barriers and problems that exist on modern ships so that they can be addressed to see how best to overcome them according to your conditions.

I know from my previous research that many senior staff would love to pass their knowledge on, but do not feel they have the support of the company or the authority to make the necessary changes. This is sad as I am sure that the support is really there for this cost-effective system but there is perhaps a break in communication between shore and ship. One Master told me he would like to have the chief officer on the bridge with him for stations but was concerned about what would happen if something went wrong up forward. He felt he would be criticised for not putting the senior officer forward and so had to protect himself as best as he could.

I can fully understand and sympathise with that Master. He wants to be a mentor but does not feel he has the support of the company to change things to achieve that and protect himself at the same time, so he maintains the *status quo*.

Having read this book, I hope that your officers may come to those of you ashore with suggestions on how best to implement mentoring on board their ships. How would you react to this? Is there an open line of communication that would allow you to discuss this and, if you agree, bring about change?

On the subject of communications, have you ever considered how important access to the internet is to the younger seafarer on board today's merchant ships? Anybody born from the late 1970s onwards in well-developed economies will be unlikely to remember a time when they did not have access to the internet or social chat rooms. It is a way of life to them and an important one. I have to be honest, these days I would be lost after a few days without internet access. But this is what happens to many young people when they join a ship for the first time. Away from home, in a strange environment, among strangers who often don't speak the same language and no access to the internet!

For those of you onboard and reading this, just think about it for a minute and then, if that situation exists on board your ship, do me a favour and at least acknowledge it with the youngster. This could make a great deal of difference in a young person's life.

For those of you ashore, think about connecting your vessels to the internet with access for everyone on board. The cost is constantly reducing and the rewards and benefits that will follow will certainly include crew morale and staff retention. Embrace the principle as important for youngsters, not as a luxury that they can do without, and then see what a difference it makes.

A good link to the internet can also facilitate mentoring. An informal internet mentoring system has recently been set up in the US. It is in the early stages but the web-based concept links mentors and candidates. Mentors list their skills and candidates choose and approach them for help.

I was interested to talk to the founder of the scheme recently who was surprised by the massive response he got from potential mentors from all around the world willing to offer help. I was not surprised at all. The creator of the scheme is not a mariner but is highly experienced in similar schemes and I think the maritime community is very fortunate that someone is willing to do this for us.

As this scheme progresses I believe candidates will be able to connect with mentors on a long-term basis and access a wealth of experience on a one-off basis, to perhaps find solutions to particularly perplexing questions if they cannot find the answers onboard. They will just need that all-important access to the internet.

I am often asked about the benefit of mentoring for shore establishments. This is quite a difficult question for me to answer briefly. Having got to this point in the book probably the best way for me to answer is by suggesting that, if you work ashore, you take a few minutes to consider what the potential benefits may be to your company.

You see, because of who I am and what I do, I primarily concentrate on the benefits to seafarers and those onboard ship, but there are substantial potential benefits to those ashore. These are a few of the potential benefits that I have come up with:

- Prevention of accidents or incidents
- Reduction in cargo claims
- Staff retention
- Increase in meaningful dialogue between ship and shore as trust and confidence builds

I am sure you can fill in a few more points.

Another way that you may be able to assist with mentoring and the transfer of experiential knowledge on board is by encouraging the learning and use of a common language. What about providing English language courses on board? These could be from a tutor, or DVD or even an online course if the internet connection on board would support this.

If you think that mentoring would help on board your ships please encourage it but do not mandate it as this can have a seriously negative effect. I am sure that the response to your encouragement will be positive, maybe not from everyone, but it certainly will make a difference.

Chapter 10

Reverse mentoring

Having got this far in the book I don't suppose that reverse mentoring needs much introduction or explanation. It is simply a reversal of roles where the traditional mentor becomes the candidate and *vice versa*. But I think the concept, although well recognised, justifies a section of its own and it ties in with the next section which deals with when it is you who needs the mentoring.

The rapid advance of technology over the last generation has brought about what is sometimes described in the offshore industry in the US as the digital/analogue divide. A good example of this is my own home. We have only owned a home computer for the last 15 years yet my children, the eldest of whom is 20, can't remember ever living without one. It is exactly the same at sea. I am reasonably computer literate but I am not an expert like so many youngsters are, therefore I can learn so much if I become a candidate and allow those who know to mentor me.

A strong word of caution here to those young candidates brimming with information who may wish to impart some of it to 'the old man'. Let me take you back to the mid-1980s when I was third officer on a brand new ship fitted with the latest technology. This included an adaptive autopilot which allowed the vessel to wander around the course line only applying helm when outside of set limits, rather than as soon as it detected the vessel was off course. This technology was supposed to save fuel but the Master hated it as it did not steer a straight line.

I was appointed to the ship three months before we departed from the shipyard on the maiden voyage and, during that time, I attended a course on how the autopilot worked, which the Master did not attend, so I knew all about it! One evening the Master was staring at the course recorder and muttering about the lousy course it was steering as it was all over the place, so I explained to him how it worked and that it saved fuel. The Master didn't say much but just switched the thing to back up and banned us from using it in adaptive mode from then on. The next day I got a severe reprimand from the chief officer on lecturing the Master on things that I didn't understand!

I gained a lot of experiential knowledge from that although I didn't realise it at the time. If only I had opened a conversation with the Master about the autopilot and tactfully given him a way out, rather than box him in a corner, I would not have had to pay the penalty. I have often wondered what happened to the concept of the adaptive autopilot as I have never seen a similar one since. Perhaps the Master was right after all?

To obtain information successfully through reverse mentoring, there needs to be a clear line of communication between the mentor and the candidate, especially if the candidate is senior to the mentor. If this is the case, then the communication needs to be instigated by the candidate in a manner that leaves the mentor in no doubt about what is required and what the boundaries are. I know this sounds a little formal and not in keeping with much of what I have said before but I think that it is very important if roles are to be reversed.

So, what about when it is me who needs the experiential knowledge? I found this one of the most difficult sections to start in this book and I have often thought why. I have come to the conclusion that it is a difficult subject to tackle because on the one hand, most people will admit that they don't know everything, although I know some who think they do! On the other hand, nobody wants to admit that they have insufficient knowledge to do their job. The worst case is if this is found out only after an incident.

Let me take you back to the beginning of this book when I took up a lot of your time explaining how I got to where I am now. I did that for a reason. Reflect on your past in the same manner. You have got to where you are now for a reason. Yes, luck and good fortune may have played a part, although I believe we make most of our luck ourselves, but you are in your position because of your qualifications and, perhaps more importantly, because of your knowledge and experience. Therefore you have a strong foundation of knowledge to build on. I do not believe you would have got to the position you are in now without this. The question is what to do now to gain the knowledge you need to continue to be safe and successful?

The first thing is for you to identify the additional knowledge you need. This is often difficult but it certainly isn't impossible. Do you remember the first time I introduced you to my 10 minute challenge in Chapter 5? I want you to do the same thing but this time identify your greatest need rather than your greatest concern. I can't say what this is going to be, and for the purposes of this exercise, I will rely on my experiential knowledge from my own career and from investigating many marine accidents.

So, let us assume for a moment that you are a newly promoted Master of an ocean-going ship. I use this scenario because many of the accidents I have investigated over the last few years have involved just such people. First, what are the most important things you have to do that you did not have to do on your own as chief officer? Please note that I have purposely ignored the day-to-day administration of the ship which, although important, is not in my opinion critical to the operation, in that if you get it wrong there can be serious danger to your crew, ship and the environment. Here are some examples of what you are now expected to do:

● Anchor the ship
● Navigate the ship during heavy weather
● Manoeuvre the ship through heavy traffic or around a channel or fairway
● Pick up and drop off pilots

These are what I consider the top four, based on my own experience, accident investigations I have undertaken and my own research. There are more and having discussed them, you will have an idea of what I am talking about and will be able to identify, and hopefully attend to, those that you have individually identified during your 10 minute challenge. So let us look at my four one by one.

Anchor the ship

Recent statistics released by the North of England P&I Club show an increase in the number of accidents occurring worldwide during anchoring (*Signals*, spring, 2010). When I served deep sea in the 1980s it was normal for the duty officer to go forward to drop the anchor. It didn't matter who it was – third officer, second officer or chief officer. I would have been deeply offended, as a junior officer, if the Master turned round to me and said he didn't trust me to go forward, it had to be the chief officer! However, more and more, that is what is happening these days.

As I mentioned in Chapter 9, I recently discussed this with a serving, experienced Master, who always had the chief officer forward for anchoring. We talked about experience and lack of knowledge and when I asked him about this, his opinion was that if something was to go wrong he would be criticised by the company if he did not have the most senior officer forward. He didn't like the situation but felt he had no choice as any incident would leave him in an untenable position with the company.

I also understand that it is a requirement in many ships' Safety Management Systems that the anchor party should be led by the chief officer. In fact, I was on a ship recently that had just received a company directive to that effect, from the marine technical department. In that directive, it stated that the chief officer had to be forward for anchoring and mooring operations. The second officer, as the second senior officer, had to be on the bridge and the third officer had to go aft.

The directive went on to state that on no account was the chief officer to be on the bridge unless being trained for promotion, when he would be taken out of the normal roster. According to the Master, the normal training period for chief officers before promotion was two months. I wonder who in the technical department wrote that directive and what prompted it? Perhaps pressure from a vetting company – I have seen that happen – or an accident or near miss. So, is there any wonder that the accident rate is increasing when anchoring?

Let us consider our Master approaching a coast in the middle of the night to anchor his ship in a small thin anchorage, lying north/south, parallel to and approximately one mile from the coast. The ship is heavily laden and of standard design. The wind is blowing quite strongly from the northeast, so the ship is approaching a lee shore and the current is running strongly to the north, up the coast, at about 2.5 knots.

This would be a fairly difficult situation at the best of times and it is conceivable that a well experienced Master would choose to stand off and wait for daylight before approaching the coast.

However, in the scenario I have envisaged, the Master is on his first voyage and has, for the past few years as chief officer, been stationed on the fo'c'sle for any anchoring operation. In accordance with company procedure the Master has his chief officer on the fo'c'sle, just as he used to be. The second officer is in the chartroom putting the GPS positions on the chart at regular intervals – so far a fairly normal scenario.

As they approach the anchorage the Master has to decide which way to swing the ship and bring her to a stop before dropping the anchor. As the wind is blowing quite strongly he chooses to swing to starboard into the wind but right across the current not realising that the current's effect will far outweigh the effect of the wind on his laden ship. She is rapidly swept to port and although the Master tries his best to avoid it, goes aground.

We have already discussed at length a way to get the chief officer experienced in anchoring the ship but what if it is the Master that lacks the experience as in this imaginary scenario? One of the keys to this sort of training and transfer of experiential knowledge is simulators. As part of my training as a pilot, I had to take the manned model course held in the UK.

This probably ranks as the most useful course I have ever done – I learned so much about hands-on shiphandling, including anchoring. For those of you not familiar with this course it involves miniature ships of various designs out on a lake. These models are perfectly weighted and powered to perform and handle like a full size ship and after just a few minutes operating them one becomes completely engrossed in their operation as if on a real ship, especially when heading for the jetty and trying to stop the thing in time!

Actually, to this day I remember an experience I had as a cadet on a steam turbine ship (it was an old ship as I am not that old!). I was on the bridge and in my designated position operating the telegraph and writing up the bell book (a rough but contemporaneous record of events). We were approaching the berth and the pilot asked for slow astern which was immediately countermanded by the Master who called for full astern. I knew immediately that we were going to hit the berth as the old lady took ages to turn astern.

We did hit it but luckily it was only a glancing blow but what great experiential knowledge for when I became a pilot and occasionally had to berth a steam vessel. I knew from my experience that I had to ring astern well ahead of when stern way was required and I am convinced that knowledge came from my experience as a 20 year-old cadet.

Similar courses are held at various maritime centres around the world and I would strongly recommend that any newly promoted, or soon to be promoted, Master be encouraged to attend one of these courses. They are quite expensive but I believe the benefit far outweighs the cost, especially if attendance prevents a costly accident. So, Master, if you think you need the training why not approach your company and ask them if you can attend a course next time you are ashore?

Once again, I have to ask the question: if you are a shipowner, manager, operator or superintendent, how would you react if a Master came to you with such a proposition? Would you encourage it and try to arrange the course or would you question why a person in such a position as Master of a vessel is coming to you with such a request? You think Masters should have the training and experience already, right? I would hope, having read this book that you would be open to the request and respect the fact that the Master has the courage and confidence to come to you and that you will act accordingly.

Navigate the ship during heavy weather

In my opinion, this is another critical operation where your actions (certainly as Master) are crucial to the safety of all on board your ship. Where do you get the knowledge to navigate your ship through the worst of weathers? I suppose the obvious answer is not to end up in that sort of weather but that is not always possible, even with today's technology. The worst weather I have ever been in was a storm in the North Atlantic in 1986. In fact it was the worst storm to occur there for 10 years and we went right through the middle of it even though we were weather routed. Sometimes it just happens!

I was third officer on a large new ro-ro/container vessel of 270 metres in length and height of eye on the bridge of 34 metres, carrying a full cargo of containers, cars and various other break-bulk items. I was up there when, according to the clinometer, we rolled 43°. Mind you, the seas were 22 metres high and a very short period as we were nearing the relatively shallow waters of the Grand Banks.

We endured 18 hours of that weather, hove to, with the Master on the bridge and the chief engineer down below, regularly having to restart the engine as it kept tripping on high revs as the propeller came out of the water as we pitched so heavily.

We survived the storm although the vessel was badly damaged, much of the cargo was destroyed and many cars had to be discharged by bulldozer and back hoe. Three people were hurt, sadly with long-term effects which affected their careers at sea. There is no doubt in my mind that our survival (a ship was lost in the same storm to the north of us and all hands perished) rested with the skill and experience of our Master who brought us through and kept us safe.

As I reflect on that storm and many others I went through, I now realise how much I learned and how I have benefitted from the experiential knowledge I gained from just watching what the Master did in those instances.

When it came to my time to get my ship safely through a storm I had a strong foundation of knowledge to rely on although, with the exception of a couple of lectures at college, I was never formally taught what to do.

If you are concerned about your ability to handle a ship in a storm please take a few minutes and reflect on all those storms you have been through and what the Master did to keep the ship and crew safe. You may be surprised at how much knowledge about what to do for the best you actually have. Couple that with what you learned at college over the years and you will find that your foundation of knowledge is strong, so build on that. There are many good books around to help you expand your knowledge and I am sure there are probably some on board. If not, ask for them to be put onboard as a reference document and for training of the junior officers. They don't need to know that you want to read it too!

If you are not in command yet but aspire to become Master, now is the time to start taking notice and learn from observation. If you go through a storm, wait until it is over, and then ask the Master to talk you through it and what was done to prevent damage to the ship. I am sure that any Master will be happy to talk about it and probably be delighted that you have taken an interest and it could lead to you finding a mentor.

Remember, you do not have to wait until you are a chief officer to have this conversation. Most Masters will happily share their experience with you whether you are a cadet, third officer, second officer or able seaman; it really will not matter to them. From time to time we all get a bit tied up with position, rank and titles.

I like to use the title Captain because that is what I see myself as, even when I was working ashore. For that, I often receive good-natured abuse from some of my engineer colleagues. This is one of the major things I like about mentoring as it naturally breaks down these barriers allowing a flow of knowledge between two individuals whatever their position. Yes, your mentor will probably be senior to you but the difference fades away when a true mentor/candidate bond forms.

Only recently, one of my mentors accidentally termed me "son" when he was sharing some knowledge with me. He was quite embarrassed by it, but it didn't bother me in the slightest. It was a moment that passed as quickly as it arrived, but I'll not forget it.

Manoeuvre the ship through heavy traffic or around a channel or fairway

Manoeuvring a ship in heavy traffic can certainly be a daunting task for our first-trip Master especially if the ship is somewhere similar to the Dover or Malacca Straits; I can remember being in the latter once and wondering how I was going to find a way through all the fishing boats that appeared ahead of me.

What made it worse that night was that the gaps where I thought there were no fishing boats were actually full of boats without lights! If you find yourselves in a similar position I would again ask you to remember all the experiences you have had with traffic in the past just as we did for heavy weather. You know what you have to do, and don't forget you are the Master now. So if you want to slow down and take a little more time to assess the situation, what is to stop you?

Now we come to the shiphandling bit and you may need to take a ship through a tight passage before you pick up the pilot. The approach to Fremantle in Australia is one, if I remember rightly, where there is quite a tight turn. In another instance I called at a port in Central America to load bananas, on my first trip as a cadet, where we had to weave our way through a coral reef before the pilot came out in a very small boat to do the last bit.

If you are a first-trip Master, I wonder how many times you have done this. Certainly you should have done it in a simulator when attending college or you may have had the opportunity to do a shiphandling course. But let us assume that you have not.

One way you can get some practice is by manoeuvring the ship at every opportunity you have and it does not have to be in a narrow channel or fairway, it can be in the open sea. Why not aim to arrive at a pilot station half an hour before your pilot time. Spend that half hour manoeuvring the ship at slow speed; try turning and see how much wheel you need on that specific ship.

Before entering port it is good maritime practice and mandatory in some places to test the steering and operation of the engine astern. This is an ideal opportunity to practise turning the ship and to assess how much the bow swings when going astern. The latter is important information to pass on to the pilot when he boards and it is great if you have first-hand knowledge to pass on.

I remember going in to one port a while ago as a junior officer with an offshore fairway that required an almost 90° turn. As we approached the turn the Master gave just 5° of wheel and the ship went around beautifully. I commented on this to the 'old man' and he just grunted something about "she doesn't need much". I have to say he was one of the most obnoxious chaps I have ever sailed with but I certainly learned something from him that day that stood me in good stead for when I became a pilot.

Another good way to assess the manoeuvrability of your ship is to perform a Williamson Turn while at sea. For those of you reading this that are not seafarers, the Williamson Turn is a way of quickly and safely turning the ship around when running at full speed, and proceeding back on a reciprocal course, primarily designed to find and recover a man overboard.

So what better excuse do you need? No one is going to criticise you for undertaking this vital safety training, are they? Do this as a drill and involve the whole team. You have a great mentoring opportunity and your action may just save a life, maybe not on your ship, but further down the line. Regrettably, people still fall off ships and maybe one of your team will know what to do because of you and just because you wanted to assess the manoeuvrability of your ship!

Pick up or drop off the pilot

I have included this section, not so much from my research and investigation of accidents, but from my own experience as a pilot. Sometimes after boarding a ship I found myself saving the Master from a horrible problem. That is not to say that accidents do not happen in pilot boarding and disembarking areas. They do, and all too frequently.

What I am thinking about here is:

- How you approach the pilot station
- How you reduce speed and make a safe lee
- What you do once pilots are onboard and before they get to the bridge

I hope by now you are getting the idea of what I am talking about, how I break down each scenario into manageable pieces and how I include a short period of reflection or assessment before any operation. I would expect that this is the methodology that you would employ if you were explaining it to someone else.

So back to picking up the pilot. When you approach the pilot station you are likely to encounter a significant amount of traffic, both inbound and outbound, all intent on getting to the same position as you! The Wandelaar pilot station for Antwerp and Vlissingen immediately springs to mind. This can be a very daunting task, especially for our first-trip Master.

One thing to remember is that you are not alone. There may be a vessel traffic management system (VTS) that will provide you with information on other vessels. The pilot station or pilot boat will call you and direct you to the position where they want you to board the pilot.

Just before you board the pilot, they will also give you a course to steer and speed to maintain. In addition, the outbound ships may have pilots on board; they will know that you are there, picking up a pilot and will direct their Masters accordingly before disembarking their ships. They may call you to let you know what their outbound ship is going to do once they have dropped the pilot.

Just a word of caution here, based on my own experience. Be very wary of outbound or inbound ships where the pilots have previously agreed a passing that is not in accordance with the collision regulations, such as a green-to-green passing rather than a red-to-red as required by Convention. You may have fully understood what was agreed but the Master on the other ship may not and, if the pilot has disembarked, may alter to pass you conventionally. A number of accidents have occurred in this way.

So, going back to our scenario, you will probably be bombarded with a significant amount of information, plus you have the safe navigation of the ship to think about and so why not get someone to assist you? The chief officer is the obvious candidate. You can probably see a pattern developing here as, once again, I advocate having the most senior officer on the bridge to assist you rather than perhaps stuck on the fo'c'sle head just in case you have to let go the anchor.

If you are ashore and reading this and in a position within a company to effect change, I hope that I have now convinced you that it is time to review your vessels' ISM procedures and ensure that the systems in place are flexible enough to allow for bridge teams to function properly and for officers to gain experiential knowledge before they move to the next rank.

If you are going to do this, please include the ship's staff in the thought and decision-making process. Remember that ship I told you about earlier that received an instruction dictating where each officer had to be for stations. The officers felt they had no choice in the matter and had to just do as they were told, which is really quite sad. The person who wrote that instruction may be far less experienced than those to whom the instruction refers.

We have already covered how to practise reducing speed and turning the vessel in the previous sections. Just another word of caution. Some ships are very difficult to slow down, so take it cautiously, whether you are a first-trip Master or hugely experienced but not on that particular ship. It is a horrible feeling, believe me, when you wonder if the ship is going to slow down in time. Much better to have to increase speed a little having slowed down too early.

Finally, once the pilot is on board it is not all over. I remember once boarding a ship at the southeast entrance to the Thames, off the UK's northeast Kent coast, in a gale. For me to safely board, we had to turn the ship towards the coast. It was quite a big ship and took me a little while to get to the bridge. As I opened the wheelhouse door I had a lovely view of the white cliffs, right ahead! The Master, unfamiliar with the area but wanting to be helpful, had increased the speed to full ahead but waited until I was on the bridge to tell him what course to steer. "Hard to port please Captain," I said.

In fact it was not uncommon for me to reach the bridge and have to take immediate action to avoid collision or grounding. It seems that occasionally officers consider that their job is done as soon as the pilot boards. A few moments of reflection on what is going through a pilot's mind when they walk through that door and looks out of the bridge window may be all it will take. As long as the ship is steering OK, if you are not sure where to head, leave the engines on a slow speed, no one is going to mind and you may avoid putting the pilot and your ship in a very difficult position.

If you experienced any difficulty while picking up pilots then, when time allows, don't be afraid to discuss this with them. Most pilots will be delighted to share their experience with you and may be able to guide you on how to adopt a better boarding position for next time. If this does happen, then please share the knowledge with the chief officer so that he won't have to experience the difficulty you did.

Chapter 11

When NOT to be a mentor

This may strike you as a strange chapter to include towards the end of a book that has exhaustively tried to convince you that it is time to start being a mentor. However, there are times when it is you that has to undertake the operation and not hand it over to a candidate.

This was brought home to me a short while ago when I was on an assignment which involved me transferring from a large ship to a tug and then back to the ship in less than ideal weather conditions. I managed the transfer to the tug OK via a pilot ladder, which for me is the best way to transfer, and did what I had to do on board so it was time to transfer back. The Master of the ship managed to make the best lee that he could as the ship was at anchor, but there was still a bit of a swell running.

The tug mate was now on duty and operating the tug's azimuth controls but I was pleased to see that the Master was still on the bridge and clearly guiding the mate. This was fine by me until the third attempt to get alongside the pilot ladder long enough for me to step over the bulwark at the bow of the tug and on to the ladder. Each time we approached we hit the ship and bounced off.

The mate clearly did not have that fine control of the tug that comes with experience. In the end I had to convince the Master to go back onto the controls and put us alongside which he did first go and I was able to board the ship safely.

I love to see people mentoring and learning how to do the job, especially when the conditions are not ideal but, when lives are at stake, that is the time that you need the most experienced person in control. In most cases that will be the Master, but not always. I have been on ships when the chief officer has far more experience than the Master and I certainly would not criticise you if you decided to leave the chief officer on the controls. But that is your decision and yours alone as, in the event of an accident, you will have to justify your actions.

Also, think carefully before putting a candidate in a position that they are not comfortable with. Watch the body language that the candidate is exhibiting – perhaps the amount of perspiration appearing or a flushed face. It may be better to step in with an apology that you didn't realise that the conditions were going to be as bad as they were, or something similar, which will tactfully allow the candidate to stand down with some dignity and hopefully not put them off for the future.

Please don't be put off when you meet someone who does not want to receive experiential knowledge. For many and varied reasons, some people just don't want to learn any more. If they know enough to do their job successfully and safely then, so be it; if they don't, then you will have to decide what to do as befits your position. Personally, I am always interested to try to find out why a person does not want to learn but you may not have the time for that. However, it may be worth spending 10 minutes finding out why, just in case!

Chapter 12

Developing a culture of mentoring

A culture of mentoring – what does this really mean? It is what I am ultimately trying to achieve in the same way as I have tried to encourage and develop a conversation about mentoring. We have now engaged in that conversation and I hope that I have convinced you of the need for mentoring at sea, as important now perhaps than ever.

Mentoring can begin with just one act which, if it goes well, will lead to another. Gradually, people will become comfortable with the concept and mentoring can take place spontaneously as a recognised action rather than something out of the ordinary.

Before too long a culture of mentoring will develop where mentoring is recognised as an ordinary but necessary action for staff to gain the experiential knowledge they need to advance or undertake their role successfully.

Please, to those of you (possibly ashore) in a position to regulate this – don't! I would ask that you encourage mentoring at every opportunity but don't be tempted to enforce it as this may lead to resistance, or worse, it may stall a process that has just begun.

Consider the effect on the maritime community if every seafarer took just 10 minutes out of their busy lives to pass on a piece of experiential knowledge to another seafarer. The effect would be huge and how many accidents might be prevented? Perhaps a life would be saved or maybe more young seafarers could be convinced to stay at sea when they were considering a move ashore to a different profession. Maybe the individual effect won't be that great, but perhaps a seafarer will tonight be smiling about their achievement today and looking forward to tomorrow.

And what is there in it for you? I am sorry, but there is no designated reward. However, as you watch the sun set tonight, reflect on the difference you have made by your action. You have passed on a piece of experiential knowledge and somebody has benefitted from that. More than that, you have done this because you wanted to and not because you had to. No one has forced you to do this and there is no form to fill in at the end, or box to be ticked. You have gone some way to restoring or creating a culture of mentoring on board; a system of transferring experiential knowledge that is as old as seafaring itself.

For me, learning is a lifelong occupation and, as Masters of our trade, I believe we have a traditional duty to pass this learning on. I also believe that the young seafarers following on after us have a traditional right to our knowledge. There is a limit to what can be taught at college and it is we who must fill in the gaps for them.

Mentoring at Sea

This is the end of the book but I hope that for you it is also the beginning. If you are already a mentor transferring experiential knowledge when the opportunity allows then may I say "thank you." Please do your best to encourage others to do the same. If you are not, then I would ask you to give it a go. If you feel that you can't, that this is just not for you, then perhaps you could still encourage others to pass on their knowledge.

One thing that I do not accept is when someone tells me that they are not in a position to be a mentor. In my opinion, there is no such position; everybody can pass on a piece of knowledge, no matter who they are or what they do. As I have said so many times throughout this book, we are all members of the maritime community and share a worldwide common bond. Together we can make a difference.

I don't have a website, but The Nautical Institute does and is very supportive of the concept of mentoring and the benefits it brings. This can be found at www.nautinst.org and I can be contacted through The Nautical Institute's online mentoring forum at www.nautinst.org/en/forums/mentoring/

I hope having read this book you will share your experiences with me, especially if it has made a difference or if there is anything you think should be included in the next edition.

Thank you for engaging in this conversation about mentoring. I hope you have found it of interest and perhaps have come to realise that you have that knowledge. Now all you need to do is pass it on!

Safe seas and clear horizons, always!

André

About the Author

Captain André L Le Goubin MA FNI

André is currently employed as a mooring Master in the lightering trade, undertaking ship-to-ship transfers in the Gulf of Mexico, having decided to return to sea in the summer of 2012 after eight years ashore working as a marine consultant in Houston, Texas.

As a consultant, he was involved in numerous salvage cases and in marine casualty investigations, including groundings, heavy weather damage, unsafe port, tanker cargo contamination and dry cargo damage. He emigrated from the UK to the USA in January 2004, leaving the London Pilotage Service where he was a first class marine pilot. This gave him a wide experience of handling and berthing a huge variety of vessels, many operating with minimum under-keel clearance.

Before becoming a pilot, André was Master of high-speed ferries (initially hydrofoils, then mono- and multi-hull ro-ro/passenger vessels, including newbuilds), operating with a variety of propulsion units.

During a period working for a Channel Island government, he undertook formal training in investigation techniques. He has also been an instructor in human behaviour and crisis management.

His seagoing career began with Cunard Shipping Services where he served as deck officer in various ranks, gaining experience of a wide variety of vessels, including reefers, tankers (both VLCC and product) and later on one of the world's largest ro-ro/container vessels on the north Atlantic trade.

He holds a current Class 1 Master Mariner (Unlimited) certificate and has recently achieved a Pass with Distinction, MA Work Based Learning Studies (Marine Accident Investigation), from Middlesex University, London. He was elected a Fellow of The Nautical Institute in 2009.

André lives in Houston with his wife and three children.